P9-APA-038

RISK AND OPPORTUNITY
A New Approach to
Stock Market Profits

RISK AND OPPORTUNITY

A NEW APPROACH TO STOCK MARKET PROFITS

CONRAD W. THOMAS

1974

DOW JONES-IRWIN, INC. Homewood, Illinois 60430

First Printing, February 1974

Printed in the United States of America

Library of Congress Cataloging in Publication Data

Thomas, Conrad W
Risk and opportunity.
Bibliography: p.
1. Investments. 2. Speculation. 3. Risk.
I. Title
HG4521.T465 658'.91'3326 73-87266
ISBN 0-87094-065-1

To
Rosy
*"The Brazilian Bombshell"**
who, during critical periods,
washed sox and performed,
with great distinction,
other essential services;
bought Xerox for pennies†
and is still holding on‡

* Romanian, actually.
† Adjusted for splits.
‡ To Xerox and, in a somewhat different fashion, the author.

PREFACE

To those now experiencing them, the economic and political troubles of the current times are only too familiar. During the writing of this book the investment world, and especially the stock market, was in disarray. Even the Securities and Exchange Commission, whose duty it is to regulate the industry, was caught up in the pervasive scandal in Washington, so that its leadership was in flux and in doubt at a time when profound changes—guided, unguided and misguided—were taking place in the nation's securities markets.

Not only political leadership but national economic planning faltered. Fiscal and monetary policies, along with an unwieldy series of decreed economic phases, led to record high rates of interest and inflation, as well as shortages of raw materials, food, and energy—in America, the Bountiful.

Stock exchange leaders and many others on Wall Street were profoundly disturbed by the illiquidity of the market, which was worsened by the flight of individual investors and virtual dominance of the market by the big institutional investors. That dominance resulted in a "two-tier" market in which only a relatively few stocks were actively pursued, while the others languished. Brokerage houses, decimated by their own bad management during the 1969–70 bear market and then hit by the 1973 market slide, were still going under.

Foreign investors in U.S. markets, hurt by two devaluations of the dollar and fearful of more to come, were deeply affected by these trends, and by deeper fears about the soundness of the nation's economy. Nevertheless, with billions of cheap dollars on hand, they were buying up U.S. property and businesses on an unprecedented scale.

Corporate officials of all but the largest companies were worried about the difficulty of raising capital for new ventures or for expansion, upon which the growth of the economy, and the welfare of all, depend.

Mutual funds, once ballyhooed as the soundest form of "people's capitalism," were then and are still suffering net redemptions, for the understandable reason that for a long time they have failed, on average, to perform as well as portfolios selected by pure chance.

As a result of the general failure of traditional investment managers, advisers and analysts, a new cult has been gaining strength which says, in effect, that you can't beat the market, so the only wise course is to abandon research, invest in the averages, and adopt a passive buy-and-hold policy. The primary target of these self-styled "modern capital market theorists" is the nearly $200 billion in pension and profit-sharing funds, so the financial welfare of millions of people, as well as the nation's economy, could be affected.

The stock market has been subjected to many abuses in the past, and evidence that the will to abuse is very much alive today can be found in every issue of *The Wall Street Journal.* Yet it is essential that a smoothly functioning stock market be restored and improved, for the alternatives are, quite simply, either state ownership or rule by the bank trust departments—fates which both business and government should work to avoid. We hope to see, after the catharsis of the American tragedy known inadequately as Watergate, some improvement in the general morality—for that is where most of our troubles, including those of the stock market, lie.

With respect to the market itself, we do not believe that the new cult of the modern capital market theorists, which we explore at some length in these pages, will do much besides confuse the issues. We do believe that investment methodology can be improved by looking at the area between current theory and practice. By introducing a few innovations, we hope to point the way toward a logical system of portfolio management and, eventually perhaps, a sounder stock market and economy.

Los Angeles, California
January 1974

CONRAD W. THOMAS

CONTENTS

1

INTRODUCTION AND APPROACH

THIS INTRODUCTORY CHAPTER outlines the major goals of the book, the growing importance of the subject matter discussed, its remarkably controversial nature, and the reasons why the author not only welcomes the controversy but does his best to add to it. The basic approach, essentially that of an experienced engineer and consultant with a deep and longtime interest in the stock market, is explained, followed by the manner of presentation, which contains hints for the reader on how to get the most from the book in the least possible time.

Goals

The main goals of this book are as follows:

1. To bridge the gap which now effectively separates stock market theorists and practitioners; that is, to provide theory and method which practical investors will find acceptable, logical, and effective.
2. To examine critically the basic tenets of modern capital market theory, including "random walk" and the "efficient market."
3. To define investment *risk* in stricter and more useful terms, separating it from investment *opportunity,* with which it is always associated.

4. To provide a number of new and useful measures for the quantification of risk and opportunity.
5. To demonstrate how these measures can be used to direct every major step in the investment decision-making process: (*a*) measurement; (*b*) comparison, screening, and selection; (*c*) timing; (*d*) monitoring and control; (*e*) maximizing return with minimum risk; and (*f*) review and adjustment; in short, to provide a logical, quantitative method of portfolio management.

Overall, our goal is to present the material in readable, nontechnical language, so that it will be easily comprehended by, and useful to, the intelligent individual investor and financial student as well as the professional portfolio manager and financial analyst.

Our approach to these goals will be that of an experienced consulting engineer with a fairly recent overlay of training in finance at a well-known graduate school of business, plus several years' participation in the stock market and, over the last few years, financial research, consulting, and writing.

The engineering approach is important, for we believe that it can be used to find the best solution to almost any problem, and certainly any problem whose raw material consists primarily of facts and numbers. To our knowledge, the engineering approach has never been applied to the stock market. This may explain both why consistently good portfolio management has proven so elusive, and also the current popularity of the so-called modern capital market theorists (modcaps). If no vacuum existed, it seems to us, these "modcaps" would have no place to go.

The modcaps define risk as uncertainty and quantify it with some measure of variability. They believe that the stock market is "efficient," that is, that securities are correctly priced at all times, having instantaneously discounted in advance all available or anticipated information—and so it is futile to try to outperform the market.

The implications for portfolio management, say the modcaps, are these: (1) select stock portfolios which will exactly equal the performance of the market itself, like the stocks of the Standard & Poor's 500; (2) follow a buy-and-hold policy as closely as possible; (3) further minimize costs by abandoning traditional research; (4) adjust risk and "expected return" by liquidating risky assets (stocks) or by borrowing: (*a*) reducing both by going from stocks into risk-free assets or (*b*) increasing both by borrowing to increase the portfolio of risky assets; and (5) don't change the risk level once it has been set.

We, in contrast, define risk as exposure to the possibility of loss, separating it from the other element of variability, opportunity, which is exposure to the possibility of gain. We derive simple formulas for measuring both risk and opportunity, and show that the market is *not* "efficient," that stocks do *not* adjust "instantaneously" to the available information, and that stocks are in fact usually either overpriced or underpriced.

The implications of *our* approach for portfolio management are: (1) the potentials for gain or loss in the stock market lie predominantly in the magnitude and frequency of price changes; that is, in measuring, and taking advantage of, under- and overpricing; (2) in order to maintain a truly efficient portfolio—one having the highest opportunity for the lowest risk—stocks should be bought when opportunity is measurably high and risk low, and sold when the reverse is true; (3) by the use of these measures in a logical system of portfolio management, any desired level of risk can be maintained, and performance can indeed exceed that of the market; and (4) fundamental analysis (while the general state of the art is admittedly low) can and must be used to arrive at accurate values for the variables needed to calculate risk and opportunity.

It may be helpful to the reader if we contrast the engineering approach to that of the modcaps. They admit to being a "cult" and to the necessity of overcoming self-doubts by becoming "True Believers" in the theory. Their approach is aptly indicated by James H. Lorie and Mary T. Hamilton, in their recent *The Stock Market: Theories and Evidence,* in which they invoke the name of a famed economist in their effort to find backing for the model upon which modern capital market theory is based. Admitting "the lack of realism of the assumptions underlying the model," and their "apparent absurdity," they come to the rescue with these words:

> Fortunately, it is now generally understood that the value of a model lies in its predictive or explanatory power and the model cannot be judged by reference to the realism of the underlying assumptions. This point has been expressed with great clarity and persuasiveness by Milton Friedman in a famous essay [in which he wrote] . . . "the relevant question to ask about the assumptions of a theory is not whether they are descriptively 'realistic,' for they never are, but whether they are suffi-

ciently good approximations for the purpose in hand. And this question can be answered only by seeing whether the theory works, which means whether it yields sufficiently accurate predictions."[42]*

No engineer will buy this line, although others might. Friedman's essay, "The Methodology of Positive Economics," sounds a lot like Dr. Norman Vincent Peale's *The Power of Positive Thinking,* written for another kind of true believer.

The "absurd" assumptions that Lorie and Hamilton are referring to are not even the ones we object to under what we call the "basic fallacies of modern capital market theory" (Chapters 16–19). *Theirs* are the following:

> . . . risk aversion; identical time horizons and expectations of all investors with respect to each financial asset; identical borrowing and lending rates; neither taxes nor transaction costs; and rational investors.

We tend to overlook these minor details in order to concentrate on the major fallacies. As for Friedman's acid test on whether the theory *works,* we show the evidence to be weak and contradictory.

Importance of the Subject

The so-called modern capital market theorists, having presented rather convincing statistical evidence to expose the general ineptitude of conventional money managers, are now enjoying rapidly widening influence throughout the investment world. Not only have their theories spread from the campus to the research staffs of institutions managing most of the country's financial assets, but they have strongly influenced the attitude of the Securities and Exchange Commission (SEC) toward the industry it regulates. In the commission's massive *Institutional Investor Study Report,*[54] the question is not whether to embody these new ideas in the regulation of such matters as reporting risk-adjusted performance and setting performance fees on that basis, but whether or not existing laws are enough to compel conformance.

Mutual funds are not the only financial organizations whose performance would be assessed according to the standards proposed by

* Numbers refer to references listed alphabetically by author in the Bibliography.

the modcaps, but also pension and profit-sharing funds, endowments and trusts, large banks and insurance companies along with the smaller but growing financial consultants. Therefore, these startling ideas, if generally adopted, will have a profound effect upon the nation's financial institutions, money markets, and economy as well as the entire population.

Besides research departments and the SEC, the modcaps have also infiltrated the upper levels of portfolio management in all sorts of organizations, from banks to pension funds. Some funds, called "market index funds," are already operating on the principle that you can't beat the market. Having declared the conventional stock analyst obsolete and laid down their own rules for portfolio management and the assessment of performance, the modcaps are coming out with books to beguile even the ordinary investor.

This is not to imply that the latter has not already had some exposure to the products of the modcaps. A "beta industry" has sprung up around their method of measuring stock market risk. Among those who sell beta in one form or another are such well-known names as Merrill Lynch, Wells Fargo Bank, Jas. A. Oliphant, Value Line, and Weisenberger Services.

In view of this wide and spreading influence of modern capital market theory, we believe that an examination of its basic tenets is in order, and we attempt this. Most of the book, however, is concerned with our own method for achieving the announced goal of the modcaps—efficient portfolio management. Because our methods differ in many basic ways, we look forward to some critical response.

A Subject of Controversy

This book will be labeled controversial; we shall present evidence in a moment to support the assertion. Those ideas put forth herein which will be considered by the modcaps controversial, if not completely mad, are, for the most part, our own (although we have been able to find some support among theoreticians who have not joined the cult). Any vituperative response these ideas incite should be directed at us—not our publisher, who, in his even-handed way, has also sponsored works by authors with whom we do not see eye to eye. (All communications, from friend and foe alike, should be mailed to Box 49471, Los Angeles 90049.)

For our part, we welcome the controversy, for we feel that it will lead to a clearer definition of terms, more effective methods for measuring risk and opportunity, and a more logical and successful approach to portfolio management—to the benefit of all concerned. Although our writing style at times may verge on the satiric and may even seem aimed at inspiring controversy, our intent overall is to seek the truth, not to alienate or infuriate.

As evidence of the controversial nature of our approach to market theory, we offer excerpts from letters received by the editor of *Barron's* following the publication of our article, "Beta Mousetrap? There's a Simple and Practical Way of Measuring Risk."[62] The article questioned, as this book questions, some of the most sacred beliefs of the modern capital market theorists. Although the majority of the reactions to our article ranged from thoughtful to enthusiastic (one reader, James Fenlon, was even inspired to write a poem about a "Better Beta" which has since appeared in *Wall Street Reports*), the reactions from the modcaps, somewhat higher pitched, ranged from incredulous to apoplectic-vituperative.

Just to cite one example here, we quote two passages from a long letter written by a pair we'll call Two Gentlemen of Denver. Following some harsh words about *Barron's* editorial policy and objectivity, the Two Gentlemen berated our "use of guilt by supposed association with such people as 'Bet a Million' Gates" (to whom we had referred casually along with Bernie Cornfeld). "This would be much like attributing to Mr. Thomas all the character and high purpose of some alcohol-crazed snake-oil salesman, who achieved his status through the use of his own product."

Interestingly, in one of their less heated passages, the Two Gentlemen criticized what they termed our argument *ad hominem,* that is, one aimed "at the man"—his passions, rather than his reason.

The Two also ridiculed what we called Morgan's Law ("The Market Will Fluctuate"), which we used to illustrate the fact that stocks can be overpriced or underpriced—which contradicts the modcaps' very basic concept that the market is "efficient," meaning that stock prices are right where they should be at all times. If our Morgan's Law concept had merit, said the Two as one, "it would predict when and how much stocks would go up or down. If Mr. Thomas can do this, then he should keep his mouth shut and act on his skills, unless he, his distant heirs, and his friends are wealthy beyond imagination."

Although other critics of the modcap persuasion expressed in varying degree their opinion that we were abusing the right of free speech, none expressed it quite so succinctly as the Two Gentlemen of Denver—and none tied our right to differ to such a high level of wealth among our friends and relatives, right down to our "distant heirs."

We find it amusing that a supposedly academic subject like risk measurement can arouse such heated passions; but of course there are sound reasons—economic, among others—for this attitude. At this point, all we ask of the reader is the willingness to believe that our subject is not a dull one.

Many of the questions raised in letters to the editor of *Barron's,* including the long letter from the Two Gentlemen, are legitimate ones; we intend to answer all of them, either directly or indirectly, before we finish.

We did, in fact, compose replies to some of our harshest critics, hoping that they would be published in *Barron's* "Mailbag," along with the critical letters themselves. We proposed also a second risk article dealing at some length with the questions raised after the first one. Due to space limitations (and God only knows what other pressures shape the decision-making process of editors), nothing appeared in "Mailbag" except two brief, rather commendatory, letters and some sorely needed corrections of typographical errors. And although Alan Abelson, *Barron's* widely followed iconoclast and managing editor, gave a favorable nod to some other pieces we suggested, his reaction to a follow-up beta article was, "let's stop while we're ahead."

For our part—in view of the considerable editing, the typographical errors, and especially the unanswered criticism—we didn't feel we were that far ahead. As to the editing, we had originally submitted two articles, titled "A Measure of Risk" (explaining our method) and "The Ten Billion Dollar Portfolio" (which applied the method to the top 20 stocks in institutional portfolios). These were eventually condensed into what emerged as "Beta Mousetrap."

None of the above should be interpreted as criticism of the editors of *Barron's,* whom we have enjoyed working with. In fact, we'll always be grateful to Abelson for reviewing the manuscript of our first book, *Hedgemanship,* and also for publishing our first article, on short selling, in *Barron's*. Would we criticize? No, indeed; we'd like to continue appearing in the magazine.

There are some advantages, however, in writing a book over writing an article, one of which we are demonstrating now: the author's freedom to elaborate on his own ideas until they are clear even to him. And, of course, to answer his critics.

Before we leave the subject of controversy, let us make two points. First, we're in favor of controversy and hope that this book will result in far more of it than did the risk article in *Barron's*. Second, our gentle twitting of the modcaps does not mean that we are against the whole theoretical approach to investment. Quite the opposite. There are many theoreticians who continue to make fine contributions to a field too long dominated by practitioners who rely on "seat-of-the-pants," "rule-of-thumb," and "gut-feeling" decision making, all anatomically somewhat remote from the brain.

Nor do we deny that the modcaps themselves have made worthwhile contributions. We do wish that they would define risk clearly, stop equating it with "uncertainty," stop pretending that the stock market is "efficient," and recognize that the terms *underpriced* and *overpriced* have real meaning. Then they will realize that current price—which they have so far ignored—is the factor which can change capital market theory from a static and esoteric concept to one which is dynamic and highly practical.

The Basic Approach

The opportunity for making money in the stock market—and the risk of losing it—depend primarily upon the magnitude and frequency of price changes. The opportunity for gain via dividends is minor compared to that presented by price increases. (Our method does, however, include a formula for assessing the effect of dividends and interest; in fact, it is the only method we know of that compares the effect of dividends to real price volatility.)

The basic method for making money in the stock market is summed up in that well-known maxim—so familiar and yet so hard to apply—"buy low and sell high." The trouble in putting this idea into practice has always been that no one to date has been able to demonstrate a consistent method for determining what is "low" and what is "high." Indeed, many empirical studies have shown (and modcap theory has been developed to support the proposition) that money managers and analysts of whatever school are wasting their time in trying to pick winners or beat the market, that is, outperform the broad market averages over time.

We disagree, ascribing mediocre performance to the lack of a logical, consistent approach to investment decision making—a deficiency which this book is meant to remedy.

The basic steps in our approach are as follows: (1) separate and define both risk and opportunity, (2) demonstrate how to measure each in terms of volatility and current price, (3) show how these measures can be used to determine when a stock's price is low and when it is high, and by how much, and (4) present a quantitative system, based upon the use of these measures, to control all of the essential steps in the investment decision-making process, so as to obtain maximum yield with minimum risk.

We have already touched on how our approach differs from that of the modcaps, and we'll elaborate, for contrast, at many points throughout the text, beginning with the following chapter, "On the Definition of Risk," where the basic divergence begins. In the final chapters, we'll take up what we consider "The Basic Fallacies of Modern Capital Market Theory."

In one of their many versions of the random walk theory, the modcaps say that knowledge of past price movements cannot help predict future price movements. This version is at least partially refuted by the modcaps themselves when they express their belief that risk (by which they really mean variability) *can* be projected on the basis of past price movements.

We believe that price *ranges,* which are essential to the measurement of risk and opportunity, can be projected with a useful degree of accuracy and that the failure of fund managers to outperform the market over the longer term can be ascribed less to immutable natural law than to lack of an effective portfolio management approach. Our position is that a nonemotional, quantitative approach based upon the risk and opportunity measures described herein (the variables of which are determined by all available relevant information) will lead to consistently superior portfolio performance.

In fact, if this approach is ever widely adopted, the end result could well be a market closer to the efficient one so dear to the hearts of the modcaps. If prices are based more upon quantified facts and less upon psychological factors, the amplitude and frequency of stock price and market swings will decrease, and investment decision making will perforce be more dependent upon true value than upon the Greater Fool Theory. With the profit potential from price swings diminished, gains by some investors will be based less upon losses suffered by others, and the emphasis will shift to the search for real value and sustained growth—to the benefit of the overall economy.

We have said that our approach is that of the engineer, but of course it is not unique to him. It is shared by the physical scientist and indeed by every individual who analyzes the available facts, minimizes emotional distractions, figures the odds, and makes his decisions accordingly.

There is even some hope for theoretical economists. An encouraging sign appeared recently in *Business Week* in the form of an article called "Optimal Control: A Mathematical Supertool."[12] According to the article, optimal control is a decision-making idea that the economists have borrowed from the engineers. It is still so new to economics that "its users have trouble defining it in non-mathematical terms." But they try: one authority describes it as "a set of mathematical techniques that tells us how to choose among alternative policies so as best to regulate or control a system."

Another, who teaches at Harvard and consults for Morgan Stanley, comments that although the economists are only just beginning to get the word, "these techniques are available, and they haven't been using them." He also says that financial management is one of the most promising fields for the application of optimal control, but he cautions that "the current state of knowledge is probably too limited to have immediate practical application."

Give them time.

Presentation

We have endeavored to write each chapter of this book in such a way that it can stand on its own, that is, so that it can be read and understood without reference to any other chapter. This necessarily involves some repetition (of matters which, by and large, can use it), but allows the reader to go directly to the chapters of major interest to him—risk measurement, say—and to skip, if he so wishes, our hassle with the True Believers in modern capital market theory. (Even the Glossary can be read independently.)

The basics of our system are explained in Chapters 5 and 13, and

Chapter 12 demonstrates some practical applications of the method. The fuller presentation ranges from Chapters 3 through 13, and applications to short selling and hedge fund operation are explained in Chapters 14 and 15. Modern capital market theorists, including random walk adherents, will probably find Chapters 2 and 16 through 19 most blasphemous; these may be skipped by readers who are not interested in the controversy.

There are no more footnotes in this book. The "superior" numbers (numbers placed above the line) indicate sources we have drawn upon in the Bibliography. Because of the controversial nature of some of our material, we have attempted adequate, but not exhaustive, documentation, mostly from the works of theoreticians. All references are listed in alphabetical order, by author's name (or by source, if anonymous). Due to the alphabetical listing, the numbers do not appear in numerical order in the text, and some are repeated.

2

ON THE DEFINITION OF RISK

CENTRAL to the thesis of this book—and also at the very center of modern capital market theory—is the definition of risk. We differ with the modcaps on this very basic matter.

Real Risk Is Exposure to Loss—and Opportunity Is Its Counterpart

We define risk as *exposure to the possibility of loss,* the sense in which everyone except the modcaps understands it. They define risk as "variability" or the even fuzzier "uncertainty about the future." Their definitions, in our opinion, have not only led to confusion about the concept of risk but also impeded the search for practical ways to measure it.

Variability should not be equated with risk because it contains both risk (of loss, if the price drops) and opportunity (for gain, if the price rises). Although risk of loss and opportunity for gain are inextricably intertwined within the factor called variability, they must be *distinguished* in order to be understood and measured.

Our definition of *risk,* then, as it applies to investing and trading in securities, is exposure to the possibility of *loss* resulting from a drop in price.

Opportunity, the counterpart of risk, is defined as exposure to the possibility of *gain* resulting from a rise in price.

(The effect of dividends and interest will be considered in Chapter 7, and short selling in Chapter 14.)

The separation of risk and opportunity, and the inclusion of *price* in the definitions of both, forms the basis for their accurate measurement—and indeed for our whole system of portfolio management.

Before turning to these matters in more detail, let's consider some ideas of the theorists on the definition of risk, with a view to both understanding their approach to measuring it and, perhaps, gaining a better insight into the difficulties they have encountered.

Although many writers on the subject of risk have exhibited, as we shall see, various degrees of unease with their definition of risk in terms of variability and uncertainty, others have taken a rather condescending attitude toward those ordinary folks who believe (along with the venerable Webster) that risk always carries with it an element of possible unpleasantness. "Hazard"; "peril"; "exposure to loss or injury" are the dictionary definitions; there is no commingling with pleasant events to dull the concept.

Or Do You Prefer Humpty-Dumpty?

One of those in the forefront of modern capital market theory, Randall S. Robinson, director of research for the Bank Administration Institute, has commented in his article, "Measuring the Risk Dimension of Portfolio Performance":

> Some individuals have been confused by the fact that risk in the popular vernacular refers to the probability of an unpleasant event while in the B.A.I. study, and in much of the research literature, it refers to how probability is distributed among all relevant events, both pleasant and unpleasant.[51]

This attitude seems not unlike that of the eminent semanticist, Humpty-Dumpty, who declared, "When I use a word, it means just what I choose it to mean—neither more nor less."

In spite of his slur upon the "popular vernacular," Robinson recognizes the problem and has even conceded that *uncertainty* would probably be a better word than *risk* when "referring to how the odds are distributed among all possible events, not just the unpleasant ones."[52] However, this concession does nothing to solve the problem, which demands the separation of unpleasant risk from pleasant opportunity in order to facilitate their measurement and use.

We said that many writers have displayed a certain unease with their own definitions of risk. A good example is to be found in "The Stock-Bond Split Decision for Pension Funds,"[31] by Robert E. Innocenti, who seems first to circle cautiously around the definition of risk, then to plunge into it as into a cold bath, and finally to retreat to a more comfortable position to think things over.

"One of the best established ideas in the theory of finance," he begins, "is that risk and expected returns are *related*. [All emphasis added] Greater risks are *associated with* larger expected returns." After declaring that the concept of expected return is a straightforward one, he says that "the notion of risk is more subtile." But in the next breath he lays it on the line: "Risk *is* uncertainty." By the next paragraph, however, caution or doubt seems to reappear: "Risk *involves* uncertainty. As the amount of uncertainty or spread of possible outcomes or returns increases, the security *is thought* to increase in riskiness." And so the retreat is complete, and the involvement of risk with uncertainty is attributed to unnamed thinkers or believers.

Actually, believers are not hard to find, but often they are just as uncertain as Innocenti about pinning down exactly what risk *is*.

Robert Levy writes:

> Risk *may be defined in terms of* rate of return. *One characteristic* which gauges uncertainty in quantitative terms is the variability of return. Available evidence *indicates* that common stock investors demand and receive a higher level of return with increased variability, thus *suggesting* that variability and risk are *related if not synonymous*.[37]

Note here again the qualifying words and phrases, with emphasis added. The last sentence also indicates the lack of precision which results when the term *risk* is used as a catchall. Risk and variability *are* related, but they are *not* synonymous.

In a recent paper, William F. Sharpe, one of the pioneers of modern capital market theory writes:

> The primary source of risk for an individual security is uncertainty about its future price. And the primary source of risk for a portfolio is uncertainty about its future market value.[58]

Lest the reader assume that there is some source of risk other than the "primary" one mentioned, Sharpe goes on to say:

> This paper uses standard statistical measures of variation to represent risk. The risk of a security is measured by a standard deviation.

He applies the standard deviation, as do most theorists, to rate of return: percentage price change plus dividend or yield. Also like many theorists, he starts out talking about price and then switches to rate of return for his risk measurement, as though the two terms were synonymous, which they are not.

A short time later, Sharpe, in a paper coauthored by Guy M. Cooper, writes that capital market theory "suggests" that "the appropriate measure of risk for a security or portfolio is the covariance of its rate of return with that of a portfolio composed of all risky assets, each held in proportion to its total value."[59]

The authors go on to say that "risk can be measured in a great many ways," and their focus at the moment is on beta, which relates portfolio return to that of the market, although "beta may not provide an adequate measure of total risk of a portfolio" unless it is well diversified.

W. H. Wagner and S. C. Lau, in discussing "The Effect of Diversification on Risk,"[70] declare:

> Capital Asset Pricing Theory states that the proper measure of risk of a security is the undiversified or systematic risk, commonly referred to as the beta of a security.

They also state that:

> The Standard Deviation is the best measure of the total risk of a portfolio, since it identifies how the investor's wealth fluctuates over time.

The foregoing examples illustrate some of the approaches theorists have adopted in their efforts to come to grips with the definition of risk. The variations, where they exist, lie mainly in the degree of hesitancy versus boldness in their definitions. Essentially, however, they are all alike; they are attempting to get a handle on risk by the use of some statistical measure of variability. It should come as no surprise, then, that the thing which all of them are talking about is merely *variability—not risk.*

More Backing for Humpty-Dumpty

Before turning to some of the doubts expressed by theorists themselves, let's consider some of the implications of the definitions of risk favored by two acknowledged authorities on the subject, the Bank Administration Institute (BAI) and the Securities and Exchange Commission.

The BAI has given lengthy consideration to the measurement of both risk and rate of return, and a group of experts under its aegis has produced some impressive volumes on these important subjects. The main report is titled *Measuring the Investment Performance of Pension Funds for the Purpose of Inter-Fund Comparison.*[40] The supplement devoted to risk measurement is called *Risk and the Evaluation of Pension Fund Portfolio Performance.*[22] A summary volume for harried financial executives was prepared by F. Byers Miller and Randall S. Robinson.[45]

The Robinson article already cited explains the institute's approach to risk in this way:

> The concept of risk is related to the uncertainty of future events. If one security is said to be more risky than another, the implication is that future values of the first security are believed to be more uncertain than future values of the second. Many different definitions of risk based upon this general idea are possible.

Also repeated here is what we consider one of the basic fallacies of modern capital market theory, based, we think, upon certain liberties taken with the statistics as well as their flawed definition of risk. Here it is:

> One of the most extensively documented propositions in the field of finance is that people can enjoy, on average, a higher rate of return by assuming more risk.
>
> Many different definitions of risk and return were used in the studies.

We'll examine this famous proposition in some detail later.

Robinson, in what appears to be a shifting of gears quite characteristic of writers on the subject of risk, follows the above remarks with this qualified statement:

> The available evidence indicates that variability in rate of return is related to risk in the short run; the longer run relationship, however, is questionable.

On the other hand, the SEC study, which we'll look at next, says: "For longer intervals the market will typically explain a higher percentage of variation in rates of return."[54] The quotation relates to the correlation between rate of return and market-related variability.)

Robinson also helpfully catalogs some of the doubts expressed by others (a subject we shall expand on presently):

> Misgivings [about measuring the risk dimension of portfolio performance] seem to fall into four categories: doubts about the definition of risk; . . . the relevance of risk; . . . our ability ever to measure risk; and . . . the adequacy of current measurement methods.

The Robinson article enumerates the final recommendations presented by the advisory committee—the faculty members, headed by James Lorie of the University of Chicago, who were responsible for organizing and writing the main BAI report. These recommendations merit quotation nearly in full, for they represent current and authoritative thinking on risk and performance measurement—basic subjects to which this book turns time and again, mostly in opposition to current theory, but with constructive intent.

The BAI's advisory committee's recommendations follow:

1. The time-weighted rate of return is one measure of the results achieved by a pension fund . . . manager. The Committee unanimously agreed that it was important also to measure the degree of "risk" taken in achieving that return.
2. A superior fund manager is one who obtains on the average a high rate of return relative to the degree of risk he has assumed . . . .
3. Its recommendation . . . is to estimate the degree of risk . . . by measuring the variability from period to period in the fund's time-weighted rate of return.
4. The Committee recommends at this time the use of the mean absolute deviation as the best measure of variability . . . computed quarterly.
5. The Committee believes that, although the recommended method will provide useful information, further experience and analysis will indicate opportunities for major improvements. For that reason, the Committee strongly recommends that further research be carried out to clarify the concept of risk . . . and to develop improved methods for estimating . . . risk.

A Somewhat Contrary View

After we have examined these propositions in some detail, the reader will perhaps agree that the final recommendation, which comes out strongly for further research and clarification, is by far the soundest.

This book will demonstrate, in fact, that (1) variability is not synonymous with real risk and is therefore an inadequate and often deceiving measure of it when comparing rates of return; (2) a superior fund manager, while striving to minimize real risk at all times, *should* embrace high variability under certain conditions; (3) measuring variability in rate of return is not a measure of real risk, and rate of return itself can be very misleading; (4) mean absolute deviation as a measure of risk can assign zero risk to a fund which is losing money steadily; and assign equal risk to two other funds, one of which is losing, the other gaining; and (5) the recommended method will provide little useful information, except insofar as it reveals its own shortcomings.

This may sound like a harsh indictment, and it is, but bear with us.

Comes Now the Securities and Exchange Commission

The SEC's *Institutional Investor Study Report*[54] was also, in all its technical aspects, dominated by modern capital market theorists. As the letter of transmittal from the commission to Congress pointed out, the study

> with its heavy emphasis on the application of quantitative, mathematical techniques to the analysis of economic and regulatory problems, has carried the Commission into new and often unfamiliar territory. No member of the Commission is a professional economist [and its] regular economic staff is relatively small. As a result, the Study's special staff necessarily operated with a great deal of professional autonomy.

These well-chosen words—which fall barely short of admitting that the commission did not really understand what the special staff of modcaps was up to, and therefore had little choice but to give the latter free rein—could also serve later to get the commission off the hook if the special staff's recommendations prove to be unworkable when incorporated into regulatory guidelines or legislation.

Nonetheless, Congress is assured that:

> The Commission, of course, has reviewed the Study's Report from its own perspective as a regulatory body. The resulting product, therefore,

represents a unique and, we believe, a constructive blend of the disciplines and the perspectives of the professional economists and the regulatory agency that collaborated in its development.

Following further disclaimers of responsibility, the commission's letter goes on to say that "we are confident that the report constitutes a valuable contribution to our understanding of this important and rapidly changing sector of the nation's capital markets."

Since we have already touched on the commission's understanding of the modcaps' efforts, let's proceed to their definition of risk and its application to the evaluation of fund performance.

Like the BAI, and indeed like all theorists to date, the SEC study equates risk with uncertainty and quantifies risk with a statistical measure of variability.

One hair-splitting footnote reads:

> Although volatility and risk are associated with one another in persons' minds, arguments can be (and have been) made that the latter (risk) is a *substantive* measure of uncertainty about possible *future* occurrences while the former (volatility) is an *objective* measure of *historical* experience. Conceptually the two can be quite different . . . . For practical purposes, however, the link between the two probably is close enough to make such distinctions unnecessary. Thus, terms such as risk and volatility, or risk adjusted and volatility adjusted can be, and sometimes are, used virtually interchangeably below [in the report].

This is the sort of "definition" that lawyers love, because it tends to assure them of full employment. The *Harvard Law Review* has in fact embraced "uncertainty" as the true definition of risk, having decided, it would seem, that the time-tested one—which implies the possibility of loss—offers too little scope for creative litigation.

The word *volatility* itself, as defined in the *Study Report,* has a meaning which, like that of *risk,* differs from the one understood by ordinary investors. These folks, addicted to the vernacular, have been using it for years simply to indicate variability in price—a meaning which should not be lost or obscured. The *Study Report,* however, in common with modern capital market theorists, applies the term *volatility* to *variability in rate of return* over selected time periods and quantifies it by some standard statistical measure of deviation or by beta, which measures only that variability which is related to the market.

The idea of measuring market-related variability is a good one, but the modcaps have complicated beta theory with such concepts (unnecessary, we think) as risk-free rate of return, and end up having to press into service another Greek figurine, alpha, in an attempt to explain the things that happen to rate of return which are not explainable by beta. It should be noted, however, that all of the measures recommended in the *Study Report,* including beta, are merely measures of variability—not real, total risk.

Nevertheless, the authors apparently believe that their partial measures of risk are good enough to serve as a basis for legislation, if necessary, requiring fuller disclosure of the risks taken by the managers of funds, including mutual funds, and also as a basis for regulating performance fees, which they feel should be determined only by "excess return." This so-called excess return would be measured by alpha rather than by total fund appreciation, which includes the market-related movement measured by beta. They don't believe that beta appreciation should be rewarded, because it is so easy to increase profits simply by taking higher risks.

Naturally, "symmetrical" penalties are in order for the fund managers when the "excess return" is negative. What we haven't found in the *Study Report* is mention of the fact that the modcaps have proved, at least to their own satisfaction, that the only way to beat the market is by borrowing to lever a portfolio whose beta is the same as the market's, and that any risk taken through what they consider to be imperfect diversification will result in a lower rate of return, and therefore negative excess return. It's almost enough to make one feel sorry for the fund managers, whose incomes, when related to the performance records of most of them, lend an alternative meaning to the term *excess return.*

Confusion Begets Confusion

How did all the confusion about the meaning of risk get started? Well, in the beginning (somewhat as in Genesis, "when the earth was without form, and void, and darkness was upon the face of the deep") appeared "Brownian Motion in the Stock Market,"[49] which compared the movement of stock prices to the random movement of very small particles suspended in solution—which physicists call "Brownian motion." Actually, the apparently random nature of price changes had been observed long before M. F. M. Osborne's Brownian motion paper appeared in 1959. However, it seemed to give a sort of scientific backing to those who suspected that neither buyers nor sellers could profit in the long run or, as we would phrase it now, that the price was always right and risk was always equal to opportunity.

Another prophetic writing which can be compared to holy writ for modern capital market theorists, and which was published even before Osborne's, was "Portfolio Selection,"[43] by Harry M. Markowitz, the "Grandfather of Beta."

Markowitz' concept of portfolio efficiency will be considered later; here we are interested in determining why the modcaps persist in equating risk with variability. In "Portfolio Selection," which was first published in the *Journal of Finance* in 1952, Markowitz wrote:

> The concepts of "yield" and "risk" appear frequently in financial writings. Usually if the term "yield" were replaced by "expected yield" or "expected return," and "risk" by "variance of return," little change of apparent meaning would result.

And so the mischief was blessed and perpetuated; ever since, Markowitz' followers have felt secure in equating risk with variance, even though Markowitz himself later hedged somewhat. As Kalman J. Cohen and Frederick S. Hammer have pointed out:

> Markowitz' use of variance, or standard deviation, as a measure of risk implies a symmetrical degree of risk aversion to returns above *and* below the expected value. This is clearly unrealistic . . . . This measure of risk does not differentiate between pleasant and unpleasant surprises. Markowitz recognizes this difficulty in his later work in which he suggests that a more appropriate measure of risk may be semivariance.[16]

Semivariance, however, is only another measure of variability and does not take current price into account, so it is only a partial measure of risk. That is why, again in the words of Cohen and Hammer, "the Markowitz approach is essentially a one-period model." His model, in other words, is not dynamic because it does not take current prices into account. The importance of current price in changing risk measurement from a static to a dynamic concept will be demonstrated in the chapters that follow.

Voltaire Said: Define Your Terms

The importance of defining the terms used in capital market theory has been emphasized by Frank E. Block, executive vice president of the Financial Analysts Federation, in his article, "Elements of Portfolio Construction":

> For a basic theory of portfolio structuring, such elements [return, risk, diversification, volatility, time horizon] must be rigorously defined, but at present they are used loosely and have different meanings to different users. Without the disciplines of both definition and quantification, they are too vague to be assembled into a formal, logical structure.[6]

This is a good statement of our own position. In fact, supplying the required answers to definition and quantification—along with providing a logical system for using them in portfolio management—is what this book is all about.

Enter the Practitioners and Skeptics

Commenting on the gap that exists between theorists and practitioners, Block writes:

> The academic community is almost uniform in the view that risk is measured by variability in rate of return, which they express in such statistical terms as standard deviation, variance, semivariance, and so on. The practitioner accepts variability of return as a *part* of risk.

We go along with the practitioners here, at least in accepting variability as a part of risk, although we prefer variability of price to that of return; and we go one step further by supplying the *other* factor which determines total risk, namely, the one based upon current price.

John C. Bogle, a man who seems to have a foot planted firmly in both the camp of the theorists and that of the practitioners (as head of Wellington Management Company, a very large mutual fund group), writes that "it is reasonable to question whether deviation is in fact a valid measure of risk." However, he goes on to accept the measure; the data he presents in a table accompanying his article, "Mutual Fund Performance Evaluation,"[9] suggest, he says, that "a fund's deviation bears an observable relationship to its performance in declining markets . . . which is in fact an expost measure of real risk."

Bogle is also a believer in beta. "There's a lot of work that still needs to be done on it," he admitted to *Institutional Investor,* "but I think beta is going to be a tremendously useful new analytical tool. It tells you things you really need to know. In a sense it is part of the technological revolution we're in."[72]

John F. Hartwell, another well-known fund manager, writing, like Bogle, in the *Financial Analysts Journal,* makes clear his disdain of the present state of risk definition and measurement:

> I am going to avoid a long discussion of risk, and the meaning and the measurement of risk, because it is a bottomless pit. Some day, I think, we may have concepts of risk which will be meaningful, but I do not think they are at hand today; which is not to say that risk doesn't exist; it is only to say that the most common concepts of risk are unvalidated and I suspect largely meaningless.[30]

Hartwell, who wrote "Performance: It's Promise and Problems" in early 1969, was soon destined to gain an even deeper understanding of risk in the impending bear market, in which he was joined, of course, by all of his fellow managers of mutual and hedge funds. (He was running three of the latter.)

Skeptics are also to be found within academia, the modcaps' own stronghold. J. Peter Williamson, professor of business administration at Dartmouth's Amos Tuck School of Business, has this to say at the end of his article, "Measurement and Forecasting of Mutual Fund Performance":

> This article has been devoid of any mention of "risk" as an element in performance measurement and the selection of a fund or investment strategy. There is so little agreement among investors as to precisely what risk is, and how to measure it, that I prefer to avoid the term when possible. I have relied on volatility as a measure of the sensitivity of a fund to the market, and hence a measure of the stability of the fund's performance over time. The reader may be willing to regard volatility as equivalent to investment risk. It is a measure that academic writers have favored as representing risk, and more professionals are coming to recognize the value of volatilities in judging performance.[76]

Williamson's article also provided more bad news for the modcaps, which we'll take up in the appropriate context. Although we've never met Williamson, we like him, not only for refusing to be overwhelmed by the modcaps around him, but also because he wrote one of the most thoughtful letters to the editor following our "Beta Mousetrap" piece in *Barron's*.

The letter, regrettably, was not published, but it was read and initialed by both editors Robert Bleiberg and Alan Abelson, before it was sent along to us for reply. (This book is the reply.) To quote two of Williamson's sagest remarks, he wrote: "Thomas is quite right on casting doubt on the usefulness of variability as risk measures . . . . He is quite right in pointing out that variability measures are not complete risk measures, and I agree with him that the risk adjusted performance measurements recommended by the Bank Administration Institute are really not very useful." To be frank, he also had some doubts about our approach, doubts which we trust will be removed by this book.

Still another skeptic about modern capital market theory, and an economist at that, is Lemont K. Richardson, with Booz, Allen & Hamilton, New York management consultants. Richardson has written a perceptive article titled, "Do High Risks Lead to High Returns?"[50] in which he puts many of the modcaps' cherished beliefs through the wringer. We'll be quoting from the article again later, but here we can note his mention of some other factors which have a bearing on risk. He cites Walter A. Morton: "The possibility of long-run impairment of capital values is the primary basis of investment risk."[46]

"Most rational investors," says Richardson, "define risk as the probability of loss over a specific period of time," and "investors tend to pay greater heed to the many factors affecting the level and trend of earnings . . . than the degree of instability in the market values and profitability." Among the factors he mentions are future level and trend of earnings and dividends, growth rate, risk premium, management, investment base, capital structure, inflation, cost of funds, labor and fuel costs, regulation, population and industrial growth, competition, supply, and technology. Although all of these factors certainly have a bearing on future prices, and therefore on risk, we wonder how many investors, including institutional fund managers and their analysts (financial, not psychiatric) are now capable of distilling this information, even when available, into a quantified measure of risk. As it happens, all of these factors, and more, *can* be taken into account in determining the very few variables needed to measure both risk and opportunity.

Richardson has been dubbed by the *Institutional Investor* "perhaps the most vocal beta critic," and he has indeed let fly at a few of the grosser pretensions of the beta brigade with language almost as free-form as some of that leveled at us by critics of our "Beta Mousetrap." In juxtaposition to Bogle's enthusiastic remarks, already alluded to, Richardson is quoted:

> These people with math and computer backgrounds . . . who think they can assign precise degrees of risk to five or six decimal places are nothing but charlatans . . . . Just because the "facts" come out of a computer . . . everyone seems to think they are true. The real fact is beta is nothing but a fad, a gimmick. It tells you nothing on which you can make a portfolio decision. In my opinion, these knaves must be driven from the temple.[72]

Right on, Richardson!

In a brief written discussion following the Robinson paper already quoted, Stephen H. Archer, of the University of Washington, made some very good critical comments about the work of the advisory committee that prepared *Measuring the Investment Performance of Pension Funds* for the Bank Administration Institute:

> Little effort seems directed precisely at measuring risk (once the academy agrees on how it should be defined).
>
> Much of our attention has been devoted to refining the measurement of risk—*primarily* as one of the measures of the *variability* in the rate of return.
>
> Perhaps not enough attention has been directed as to whether it is variability in the rate of return that we should be "zeroing in" on.[51]

Archer's shafts were well aimed, but they have been ignored or deflected by the modern capital market theorists, who persist in their belief that risk is uncertainty is variability is Truth.

Archer also displayed doubts about the perfection of perfect markets and released a shaft of light upon the possible opportunities inherent in *dis*equilibrium conditions—another way of saying what this book is about.

To sum up: all of the True Believers in modern capital market theory we have quoted, and all those we know about, equate risk with uncertainty and quantify it with some measure of variability.

They differ mainly in the degree of unease or arrogance they exhibit in living with their definitions of risk. Other thinkers, less bound by the modcap dogma, have expressed various degrees of skepticism. We'll see that the doubts of the latter are well founded.

Back to Real Risk and Opportunity

It is unfortunate that in so much of the literature on risk research the word *risk,* as we and most other nonmodcaps understand it, is not real risk. In reading such literature, therefore, and also while reading the material quoted in this book, it would be well to substitute mentally for *risk* some such word as *varisk,* to represent the concept of the risk associated with variability, which is only a partial measure of total risk. Much of the basic literature, in fact, would become more useful and understandable if it were amended in this fashion.

We'll close this chapter, as we opened it, with the definitions of risk and opportunity used throughout this book in developing our quantitative method of portfolio management.

Risk, as it applies to trading in securities, is exposure to the possibility of loss resulting from a drop in price. Opportunity is exposure to the possibility of gain resulting from a rise in price.

3

RISK AND OPPORTUNITY

EVEN IN later editions of their book *Security Analysis*[27] (long and rightly considered the bible of the fundamental analysts), Benjamin Graham and David L. Dodd never bother to *define* risk, although they are much concerned with *avoiding* it—much as one might seek to avoid sin, without thinking it necessary to define *it*. Neither do they mention uncertainty as the equivalent of risk or statistical variability as a means of measuring it. These concepts—now central to modern capital market theory—originated with economists and mathematicians, not with astute thinkers about the stock market typified by Graham and Dodd.

Instead of enshrining these concepts as they now stand and confining most effort to their embellishment by means of more refined models and empirical studies, we would like to see the capital market theorists recognize that variability is not a complete measure of risk or even a dependable approximation of it. They could then turn their brainpower, human and mechanical, to more meaningful and useful models and studies.

Up until now, in our opinion, the modcaps have been merely nibbling around the edges of one side of the important subject of risk. Risk cannot be measured by variability alone, whether of rate of return or of price. As every investor knows, but the modcaps deny, current price is also important. Moreover, variability—which is certainly an important factor of risk—also contains its opposite, opportunity.

The Chinese Had a Word (or Two) for It

Risk (of loss) and opportunity (for gain) are as intimately intertwined as the yin and yang of Chinese philosophy. Although they are opposites (like anode and cathode, plus and minus), yin and yang are both essential elements in the functioning of the whole. (Symbolically, the Chinese expressed the concept with the same black-and-white intertwined circle later used by the Technocrats—if your memory goes back that far). In the philosophy, the two principles of yin (negative, dark, feminine) and yang (positive, bright, masculine) interact to influence everyone and everything. (We don't propose here to get involved in any current hassle over women's liberation or minority rights; those who would can take it up directly with the Chinese.)

We can readily appreciate the utility of yin and yang as a way of thinking about the stock market, identifying bear movements with yin and bull movements with yang, and similarly classifying loss and gain, dividend cuts and increases, and so forth.

Although risk and opportunity are as intertwined as yin and yang, each can be distinguished, defined, and measured—and in fact each *must* be distinguished and defined before it can be measured usefully. The concept of opportunity (yang) is even more important than the concept of risk (yin), for the former is the positive element of investment—the goal every investor is seeking—the possibility of gain. Risk, on the other hand, is the negative element—the thing everyone wants to avoid—the possibility of loss.

Only after opportunity and risk are defined and quantified can a logical approach be formulated for the realization of every investor's goal—maximum gain with minimum risk. (This is also the modcaps' goal with their "efficient portfolios," but they'll never get there until they learn to distinguish the yin from the yang; at the present time they're calling everything yin.)

Within the framework of risk and opportunity, the concepts of risk-aversion and efficient portfolios take on a more precise and useful meaning than in current capital market theory. When they speak of risk-aversion, the modcaps are really talking about an aversion to variability in some rate of return, which is itself—as they describe and use it in their various ways—a theoretical statistical convenience which seldom or never describes any investor's actual return. And when they speak of an efficient portfolio as one which has maximum expected return for a given level of risk, they are actually talking about expected rate of return in the rather unrealistic way they have formulated it and about risk as measured solely by variability in that rate of return.

The modcaps' concept of the risk/reward tradeoff (really variability/expected rate of return) could well be replaced by one of real risk/opportunity, the elements of which are true counterparts—not the mere variability of one unrealistic factor defined in terms of the other.

Real risk, then, as it applies to trading in the real stock market (as opposed to the efficient or perfect market of the modcaps) is simply exposure to possible loss due to a drop in price; and the exact counterpart of risk is opportunity, exposure to possible gain due to a rise in price.

Looking ahead for any period of time—let's take a year—every stock will fluctuate between some maximum and some minimum price (which forever after will be frozen on the bar charts and readily identified as the high and the low for the period). The difference between the high and the low is termed the *range,* the simplest measure of variability known to statisticians. When the range is divided by the average (the simplest measure of "central tendency" known), the result is what we have called *range variability.* It is a good, realistic, readily understood, simple measure of price volatility.

Volatility can be bad and it can be good; that is, it is part yin, part yang. A stock with low volatility will not present much risk, because no matter what price you pay, it won't drop much from there; on the other hand, it probably won't gain much either. A highly volatile stock, in contrast, can make you a lot of money on your investment or hand you a big loss.

Volatility is not all bad or all good, except when the price of the stock is at the high or the low. If you buy at the high, the price has nowhere to go but down, so volatility is all bad (risk). And, of course, if you buy at the low, there's nowhere to go but up, so volatility is all good (opportunity).

At all price levels in between the high and the low, volatility is a yin-yang mixture of risk and opportunity. Exactly how much of each exists depends upon the price at any particular time. That is why volatility by itself is not a complete measure of risk; volatility must be adjusted for current price. (A simple formula for calculating both risk and opportunity, based upon the concepts just mentioned, is developed in Chapter 5. The reader may look at it now if he wishes; we are progressing, like integration, with all deliberate speed.)

Many readers may well wonder why we have discussed these simple facts about volatility and price in such detail; after all, everyone already knows what volatility is and that it's better to buy low than buy high. Everyone, that is, except the modcaps, as we'll see.

Mr. Espresso Protests to Barron's

In our *Barron's* article on risk, we said:

> No volatility gauge alone is a complete measure of risk. It is obvious that the higher the current price of a stock, the greater its risk. This applies not only when considering the purchase of a stock at a particular time, but also to every stock in the portfolio regardless of the price at which it was purchased.[62]

A letter addressed to the editor soon arrived from an indignant True Believer, a man we'll call Amerigo Espresso to protect his identity, for his name is nothing like Italian, and we have no wish to cast any aspersions on him, the well-known company for which he toils in investment management, or the well-known financial publications which have found room for his writings. We don't mind aspersing, just a little bit—because everyone does and they've come to expect it—the well-known institution that granted him a master's degree in business administration, Harvard.

Wrote Mr. Espresso:

> Rarely has *Barron's* published an article as weak as Conrad W. Thomas' "Beta Mousetrap?" Where is the proof that "It is obvious that the higher the current price of a stock, the greater its risk?" On the contrary, virtually all the statistical work done on this subject in the last few years indicates current prices of stocks tend to properly discount all public and anticipated information—today's price is irrelevant to future risk.
>
> If Mr. Thomas accepts the Bank Administration Institute's conclusion "That investors, on average, can receive a higher rate of return by assuming greater risk" how can he pretend to distinguish between risk and opportunity? Risk *equals* opportunity—investors are paid to assume risk and there are no free rides.

Finally, Mr. Thomas claims it is logical to assume that a stock will tend to return to its average price due to "Morgan's Law" and "its corollary." Can he offer *Barron's* readers any statistical proof of this or either of his other unsupported assumptions? If not, his risk measurement techniques appear valueless.

We have quoted Mr. Espresso's letter in full, not only because it is a good exposition of some of what we call the fallacies of modern capital market theory, which has many True Believers like Mr. Espresso, but because it also demonstrates the dogmatic quality of thinking encountered by anyone who tries to introduce a new idea, no matter how simple, into their moated citadels. Their vision seems to blur after reading the first lines from the infidel.

Yes, Mr. Espresso, There Really Is a Morgan's Law

Because it was representative of modern capital market theory, we thought Mr. Espresso's letter deserved both publication and a reply, so we mailed ours to the editor; regrettably, neither was published. Some excerpts from our reply follow. (We hope Mr. Espresso will excuse the delay.)

If Mr. Espresso's reading of my article has led him to believe, as he does, that I accept the BAI's conclusion that investors, on average, can receive a higher rate of return by assuming greater risk, it is easy to understand how he has arrived at so many other erroneous conclusions. My thesis, of course, was precisely the opposite: that investors can *not* receive higher returns simply by taking greater risks; that current or purchase price must be considered along with variability. My endorsement of their conclusions, and that of other researchers with the same belief, applied only to their apparent scientific backing for the Greater Fool Theory. As the article put it: if profitability increases with risk, it follows that the riskier the deal the more the next sucker should be willing to pay for it.

In reply to Mr. Espresso's contrary view to the statement that "It is obvious that the higher the current price of a stock, the greater its risk": We thought it was obvious, but let's cite an example for Mr. Espresso. During a recent week Syntex varied in price between 83 and 89. Certainly current price mattered to those who bought the stock during the week. Buyers at 89 were risking $6 a share more than those who bought at 83. Isn't that obvious?

Does Mr. Espresso really need statistical proof of Morgan's Law ("The Market Will Fluctuate") or the fact that buying low and selling high (which our measures can help accomplish) will attain statistically better results than ignoring current price? Yet he contends that "today's price is irrelevant."

Another statement which gropes for the limits of meaninglessness (and which is well imbedded in modern capital market theory) is that "current prices of stocks tend to properly discount all public and anticipated information." Apparently, he really believes that the ideal market of the theoreticians (in which capital markets are in equilibrium and current prices of all securities faultlessly discount their expected streams of dividends and earnings) has arrived. Not yet, Mr. Espresso.

Finally, Mr. Espresso's insistence that "risk *equals* opportunity" regardless of the purchase price of the stock would seem to be a good argument against investing in the market at all, especially after brokerage and management fees are considered. As for "statistical proof" of my "unsupported assertions," the article was not without supportive illustrations, as a less agitated reader would have observed.

We'll have more to say about the modcaps' own "statistical proof" in later chapters.

As we mentioned earlier, the normal investor with some experience in the stock market knows that our position is simply common sense. However, if you happen to be a modern capital market theorist and start out by defining risk as variability, you'll never be able to separate the yin from the yang, the good from the bad, the risk from the opportunity.

Common Sense Impugned

Having put in a good word for common sense, we must warn that the modern capital market theorists have risen above all that twaddle, too. We have learned that one of them, in a book to be issued about the same time as our own, contrasts the wisdom of the collected works of the researchers cited in his book in support of "the new science of investment" based on modern capital market theory with what he calls the "diametrically opposed" intuitive approach of all non-modcap practitioners in the stock market. He illustrates his point with a parlor-trick example which tends to equate common sense with faulty reasoning.

We, too, are against seat-of-the-pants decision making and very much in favor of the scientific approach, but we suggest much more probing of "the new science of investment" before embracing it and abandoning common sense. And any science, new or old, which does not recognize that purchase price has an important bearing on risk had better take a hard look at itself.

Current price, in fact, is the missing element in modern capital market theory, and the one which, when recognized, makes possible the quantification of risk and opportunity. This theme will be developed in the chapters following.

4

PRICE IS THE KEY

In chapter 1, we stated that one of the main goals of this book would be to try to bridge the gap which now exists between the theorists and the practitioners; that is, between those who think about stocks but hardly ever touch the stuff and those who handle the stuff every day but hardly ever (according to the theorists) think about it very effectively, judging by their performance records.

Current Price: The Dynamic but Neglected Factor

Although our goal may sound like an impossible dream, much of it could be realized if the modern capital market theorists would simply accept what every practitioner knows—that current price is of critical importance, that is, that the terms *underpriced* and *overpriced* have real and very practical meaning. The very essence of capable portfolio management, in fact, depends upon the manager's recognition of, and reaction to, states of *dis*equilibrium (although he may not state the idea in exactly the same words).

In an excellent summary of the differences which separate academicians and practitioners, Block has written that:

practitioners cannot agree with those academic views which assume the presence of markets which are "in equilibrium" and "efficient markets" . . . . Either concept would tend to support the random walk adherents' belief that investment analysis can obtain no better than random results without inside information or other special advantages.

The practitioner's attitude is . . . that investors have different amounts of information, different abilities to interpret it, and different degrees of conviction and motivation.

The portfolio manager does not want to escape the unique characteristics of his portfolio holdings; he wants to participate in that uniqueness—that is why he purchased those particular securities.[6]

Block makes no specific mention in the above of favorable purchase price, but that can certainly be one of the most desirable "unique characteristics" about a stock, and one which portfolio managers are always seeking.

Block does put his finger on the difficulties besetting the practical application of the efficient portfolio concept deriving from Markowitz and his followers:

It is not hard to imagine the designing and construction of an "efficient portfolio" at a specific point in time. Yet, the moment either prices or expectations change, one no longer has a perfect portfolio. Purchases and sales would have to be made continuously . . . .

There! He has finally, perhaps inadvertently, said the key word: price. *Current price* is the factor to which capital market theorists have closed their minds—the one factor needed to change their theory from a static to a dynamic one.

That is why we have insisted upon defining risk and opportunity in terms of possible decrease or increase in price *from where it is now.* That is why we have insisted that risk and opportunity can be measured only if current price is considered along with volatility. And of course that is why there is a current price factor in the formulas we have developed to measure risk and opportunity.

In his article, which appeared in the *Financial Analysts Journal,* Block never states unequivocally—as we do—that current price is the missing factor. While discussing the various factors affecting volatility, he names quality, earnings volatility, floating supply, trading volume, market psychology, faddism, and impact of transactions triggered by market technicians. Apparently as an afterthought, he adds, "Price is also a factor since the floating supply tends to change with price." He does, however, recognize that something is missing:

A number of investment organizations have attempted to test Markowitz' theory (and Sharpe's simplification). It would appear that most of these efforts have encountered difficulties because of the aggregation of all risks into a single term—the variability of rate of return.

Block's words, we think, are enhanced by the fact that his article obviously draws upon experience as both theoretician and practitioner: as executive vice president of the Financial Analysts Federation and on the staff of the Girard Bank of Philadelphia, which we understand is a profit-seeking organization.

Price Range vs. Rate of Return

It is interesting to speculate on why the modern capital market theorists have avoided the dynamic factor, current price, and concentrated on variability in rate of return. Our guess is that they are hoping to find something that will hold still for them. Like many scientists, perhaps, they think that by repeated and ever more accurate measurements they will be able to nail down, once and for all, the precise risk of General Motors or Xerox, much as a physicist would determine the speed of light or the half-life of carbon-14.

Block has bad news for them: "the return provided by changes in market value are subject to wide swings, and cause most of the variability in rate of return which the academicians abhor."

But the modcaps still long for "stationarity," which allows them to project historical variability into the future. (See, for example, Robert A. Levy, "On the Short-Term Stationarity of Beta Coefficients."[37]) Modern capital market theory depends, in fact, upon such stationarity, and there is virtually no limit on how far back the search can go to find it. In their paper, "Using Portfolio Composition to Estimate Risk,"[68] Jack L. Treynor, William W. Priest, Lawrence Fisher and Catherine A. Higgins write, "The price history of each common stock [in the portfolio studied] was traced back as far as conveniently possible—in some cases up to 40 years." Even though they applied "exponential smoothing techniques with arbitrary weights" to their data, we can't help wondering about the weights assigned 40 years back relative to the latest year.

The authors own up to what they correctly term their "dilemma":

> If we confine our samples to very recent data, possible error due to random fluctuations may be excessively large . . . [but if] we include . . . a longer time span we may be including data which are no longer relevant because of changes in the risk character of the common stock in question.

Although they concede that "The risk character of a company's common stock may change quickly," their "scheme assumes that risk parameters for individual common stocks change relatively slowly." Obviously, they want the cursed parameters to stop all that jumping around and settle down to some dependable state of variability so that they can conclude, as they ultimately do anyway, that "our risk-measuring technique is producing numbers which are both meaningful and useful."

A handier statistical technique for realizing one's desires consists of discarding data from time periods which tend to disprove one's thesis. This approach will be demonstrated later, when we look at some of the basic fallacies of modern capital market theory.

Returning to the paper by Treynor et al., we have an example of a fairly common practice among writers on the subject of risk to start out talking about *prices* and then shifting to *rate of return* as they get down to the business of measurement:

> In recent years a number of financial scholars have commented on the marked degree of co-movement in the prices of securities . . . . Perhaps the best known model of stock prices which recognizes and incorporates the co-movement phenomenon is that of William Sharpe. In Sharpe's model fluctuations in the price of a particular stock have two causes: (1) fluctuations in the general market level and (2) fluctuations unique to the stock in question.

Following their statement that price fluctuations are the sum of (1) and (2) above, comes the switch from price to *parameters based upon rate of return:*

> The risk character of the stock is completely specified . . . by . . . two parameters; . . . sensitivity of the stock to market fluctuations [and] the average magnitude of the residual fluctuations [the part left unexplained by market fluctuations].

Instead of measuring these two parameters, termed "market variance" and "residual variance," in relation to rate of return, as is the custom of capital market theorists, we believe that it would be far more useful to go back to what most of them start out talking about: *price.*

Oldrich A. Vasicek and John A. McQuown, in "The Efficient Market Model," seem to have considered the idea, only to reject it:

> To measure risk directly as the variability of price changes is not quite convenient, since it would mean that risk depends on the *level* of the price—the higher the price in dollars per share, the higher the dispersion. To avoid this "scaling problem," variability of the rates of return is used. Another reason for choosing rates of return rather than price changes is that rates of return include dividends.[69]

There is no "scaling problem" if percentage price changes are used (exactly as they are in rates of return); and the inclusion of dividends only adds to the confusion, because it adds an element whose variability is unrelated to price change in the total rate of return.

Range Variability

This subject will be treated in more detail in the next chapter; the brief discussion here is meant to emphasize the importance of price.

Market sensitivity can be measured most readily simply by comparing the *range variability* of a stock or portfolio with that of the market. (Range variability is the difference between the high and the low divided by the average price.) In a *Barron's* article,[62] we dubbed this the "Poor Boy" beta, because its calculation requires neither access to a computer nor even the ability to distinguish between multiple regression and recidivism.

By plotting a series of stock or portfolio range variabilities (on the vertical axis, say) against those for a broad market index (measured on the horizontal axis), one can obtain as gaudy a scatter diagram as any beta theorist could want. Having done this, it is a simple matter to draw in the best-fitting straight line (those who have computers can regress in the usual fashion).

The slope of the line is *market-related price volatility.* A slope of 1.0 indicates the same volatility as that of the market; a steeper slope (over 1.0), more volatility; and a gentler slope (under 1.0), less volatility. Dispersion of the points around the slope line can be called *nonmarket-related price volatility,* and the statisticians can have a field day measuring the degree of dispersion with standard deviation, variance, and so on.

More on Price Range vs. Rate of Return

A simple example will illustrate how much more useful it is to use price range rather than rate of return (defined as ending price for the period less starting price plus dividends, all as a fraction or percentage of starting price).

By considering only two prices—only those at the start and finish of the period—all of the price history in between those two points is ignored. Let's say the stock started at 50, ended at 50, and paid no dividend during the period. Under these conditions, the rate of return, the modcaps' basic tool, is zero. But the price may have dropped to 10 in between dates, or soared to 100, or both; there's no clue in the rate of return. (The statistician may try to overcome this difficulty by taking many shorter time segments for observation, but the same objections still apply to the shorter periods; and the concept of rate of return means less and less as the periods are shortened.)

Range variability (RV), on the other hand, can yield much more information. Consider the three cases mentioned: (1) price starts at 50, drops to 10, and ends back at 50; RV = (50 — 10)/30 = 1.33, meaning that the price fluctuated 133 percent around its average; (2) price starts at 50, rises to 100, drops back to 50; RV = (100 — 50)/75 = 0.67; (3) price starts at 50, ranges between 10 and 100, ends at 50; RV = (100 — 10)/55 = 1.64. These figures, even without any adjustment for current price, are far more descriptive measures of risk than is rate of return.

(The method of calculating the current price factor is simple enough, as we'll show in the next chapter, where we derive the basic formulas for risk and opportunity.)

Another advantage which price range variability has over that based on rate of return is evident when we start comparing stocks and portfolios with the overall market. Using the rate of return method, the market itself is delineated by only two points, those at the start and the finish, which means that the standard itself is very incompletely described. Furthermore, a stock might easily be out of phase with the market—lagging or leading it—on the terminal dates, which of course are selected arbitrarily.

All in all, then, the use of range variabilities rather than rates of return when making comparisons among stocks, portfolios, and market indexes is clearly superior.

Although rate of return is a useful and indeed indispensable way to measure portfolio performance from time to time, we question the lumping together of dividends and appreciation (or depreciation) into a single measure of variability, then equating this with risk. Dividends do not have at all the same degree of variability as price changes. Combining them even tends to frustrate the modcaps' quest for "stationarity," for they're not just counting the apples with the oranges; it's more like counting the peanuts with the casabas. Even in those cases where dividends may be comparable in size to the price change, the two have different degrees of variability.

Nevertheless, the theorists include dividends with price changes in what they define as "market-related" risk, classifying other risk as "company related" (sometimes further subdivided into "industry related" or "God only knows"). Compared to prices, dividends remain relatively stable (except for dramatic cessations or lapses), and they are much more closely related to company and industry factors than to the overall market. So why have the modcaps put dividends into beta, their market-related measure of risk?

Summary

If we can convince the theorists of the truth of the above, namely (1) of the superiority of price volatility over variability in rate of return and (2) that risk due to volatility must be modified by current price (we're sure the practitioners will go along on both scores), then we will have accomplished the major part of our announced goal of bridging the gap between the two groups.

(We don't really think that the modcaps are going to suddenly stop being True Believers, but we have high hopes for the freethinkers among the academicians.)

5

MEASURING RISK AND OPPORTUNITY

RISK has been defined as exposure to the possibility of loss due to a drop in price. The simplest measure of risk is price itself. A certain stock is selling for, say, $70 a share. If you buy it at that price, the most you can possibly lose is $70, even if the company goes broke.

But hold on!—you say—that company is not about to go broke. I've been watching it; its earnings are holding up well, and its price has never dropped below 40, even during the bear market lows of 1970. Even if another bear market comes along, the price won't go below 40, so I can't lose more than $30 a share.

You are right, of course, *provided* your assumption is true (as it often is) that *past* price range is a good guide to *future* price range. The same line of reasoning can be applied to the stock's high, which has never gone above 100, say, in the hottest bull market. Therefore, the most you can *make* on the stock is $30 a share, if it hits its old high again. (Important note: We'll consider later and in detail *projecting future highs and lows,* a much more difficult task than taking those from the past, but the basic formulas developed here apply to both situations.)

Investment risk should always be considered along with investment *opportunity,* which is exposure to the possibility of gain due to a rise in price.

Range Variability

The difference between the high and the low is the *range,* the statistician's simplest and most understandable measure of variability. The range for our stock is 100 minus 40, or 60. Expressed as a fraction of the average price, 70 (midway between the high and the low), the *range variability* is 60/70, or 0.86. A range variability of 0.86 means that a stock has a price range of 86 percent of its average price. In other words, it can rise 43 percent above its average and fall 43 percent below it, and you can expect to gain or lose that amount if you buy at the average price, 70, and sell later at the high or low.

Current Price Factor

However, if you buy at a higher price—80, say—the risk is greater and the opportunity is less, because you are risking an additional $10 a share against a possible loss of $40 if the stock again hits its low.

Likewise, if the stock is purchased below its average price, the possibility for gain is greater than the possibility of loss.

Current price, then, is an important factor in both risk and opportunity.

The Risk Formula

The problem is how to measure, or quantify, risk and opportunity when the price is above or below the average price. Figure 5–1 pictures the critical prices of a theoretical stock: the high, H, the low, L, and the present price, P. In the illustration, the present price is above the average price, $\frac{1}{2}(H + L)$. The possible loss—the difference between present price and the low—is seen to be composed of two segments, the possible drop from present price to average price, equal to $P - \frac{1}{2}(H + L)$, and the possible drop from average price to the low, equal to one half the range, or $\frac{1}{2}(H - L)$. The total possible loss is therefore equal to $\frac{1}{2}(H - L) + P - \frac{1}{2}(H + L)$.

This formula as it stands could be used as a measure of risk, but in order to relate both components to the average price, we multiply through by the factor $2/\frac{1}{2}(H + L)$. Our measure of risk, then, is:

$$\boldsymbol{R} = \frac{H - L}{\frac{1}{2}(H - L)} + 2\,\frac{P - \frac{1}{2}(H + L)}{\frac{1}{2}(H + L)}$$

FIGURE 5–1
Measuring Risk and Opportunity Based upon Price

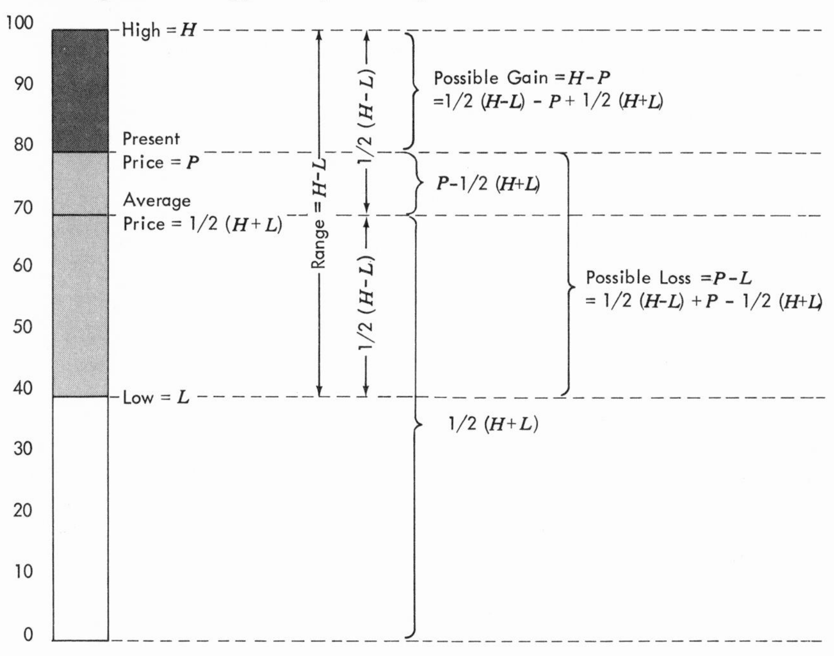

To express the formula in words: Risk is equal to range variability, RV (the first term), modified by the current price factor, CPF (the second term), which measures the deviation of the current price from the average price.

The formula looks even simpler when it is put into words:

$$\text{Risk} = \frac{\text{Range}}{\text{Average price}} + 2\,\frac{\text{Current price} - \text{Average price}}{\text{Average price}}$$

The Opportunity Formula

Referring to Figure 5–1 again, the measure of opportunity is developed in similar fashion:

$$\boldsymbol{O} = \frac{H - L}{\frac{1}{2}(H + L)} - 2\,\frac{P - \frac{1}{2}(H + L)}{\frac{1}{2}(H + L)}$$

The formula for opportunity is exactly the same as that for risk, except that the connecting sign between the two terms is minus instead of plus. In other words, a high price increases risk but decreases opportunity, while a low price decreases risk and increases opportunity.

Sample Calculations

In the earlier example, the range variability was shown to be 0.86. Selling at 70, the average price, the stock's risk is equal to its RV, because the CPF is zero. For the same reason, opportunity also equals 0.86. Only when a stock is selling at its average price does risk = opportunity = range variability. At all other times, the three values are different.

In the example, with the stock selling at 80 (10 above the average) the CPF $= 2 \times (80 - 70)/70 = +0.29$, so:

$$\text{Risk, } \boldsymbol{R} = 0.86 + 0.29 = 1.15$$
$$\text{Opportunity, } \boldsymbol{O} = 0.86 - 0.29 = 0.57$$

However, if the stock's price dropped to its previous low, 40, the CPF would be $2 \times (40 - 70)/70 = -0.86$, and:

$$\boldsymbol{R} = 0.86 - 0.86 = 0$$
$$\boldsymbol{O} = 0.86 + 0.86 = 1.72$$

And at the high, 100, CPF $= +0.86$:

$$\boldsymbol{R} = 0.86 + 0.86 = 1.72$$
$$\boldsymbol{O} = 0.86 - 0.86 = 0$$

Risk and opportunity, then, move in opposite directions from zero to a high value which is double the range variability. This statement is true for all stocks, so it is easy to see why more volatile stocks carry the most opportunity as well as the most risk.

Theoretical Limits

It is interesting to examine the theoretical limits of volatility, risk, and opportunity. Measured by the formulas, a stock selling at its high, and which can drop to a theoretical low of zero, has a risk of 4 and an opportunity of 0. With the stock selling at its average price, risk and opportunity both are equal to 2, the maximum theoretical value of range variability. At a low of zero, opportunity is 4 and risk 0. For stocks selling above zero, opportunity is always less than 4, but risk is zero for any stock selling at its low.

Zero risk? As long as a stock is selling above zero, isn't an investment subject to *some* risk? Yes, of course—but remember our assumption: that the price of the stock would not escape its range, based in this case on its historical limits. If the assumption is true, it follows that there is no risk at all in buying a stock at its low.

More Examples

The above point is most easily confirmed through the use of 20/20 hindsight. In 1972 Monsanto traded between a high of 57¼ and a low of 46. For the year, therefore, while the stock was trading at 57¼, the risk in buying it was at a maximum, while the opportunity at that price was zero. In contrast, a buy at 46 represented zero risk and maximum opportunity, because the stock had no place to go but up from its low.

In order to illustrate the simple mechanics of calculating risk and opportunity values with an actual stock, let's examine the situation which faced a potential investor at the end of 1971, when Monsanto closed at 48⅞. Let's assume that the investor was able to estimate the subsequent high and low which actually occurred (we'll consider forecasting methods in some detail in later chapters).

At a price of 48⅞, Monsanto had a risk of:

$$\boldsymbol{R} = \frac{57\tfrac{1}{4} - 46}{\tfrac{1}{2}(57\tfrac{1}{4} + 46)} + 2\,\frac{48\tfrac{7}{8} - \tfrac{1}{2}(57\tfrac{1}{4} + 46)}{\tfrac{1}{2}(57\tfrac{1}{4} + 46)} = \frac{11\tfrac{1}{4}}{51\tfrac{5}{8}} - \frac{5\tfrac{1}{2}}{51\tfrac{5}{8}}$$

$$\boldsymbol{R} = .218 - .107 = .111$$
$$\boldsymbol{O} = .218 + .107 = .325$$

With opportunity nearly three times risk, Monsanto looked like a good buy at 48⅞ (always keeping in mind the time horizon of one year or less, and the expectation of selling when the stock became well overpriced, unless new estimates of risk and opportunity at that time indicated further gain potential).

At its high, 57¼, Monsanto's risk and opportunity were:

$$\boldsymbol{R} = \frac{57\tfrac{1}{4} - 46}{\tfrac{1}{2}(57\tfrac{1}{4} + 46)} + 2\,\frac{57\tfrac{1}{4} - \tfrac{1}{2}(57\tfrac{1}{4} + 46)}{\tfrac{1}{2}(57\tfrac{1}{4} + 46)} = \frac{11\tfrac{1}{4}}{51\tfrac{5}{8}} + \frac{11\tfrac{1}{4}}{51\tfrac{5}{8}}$$

$$\boldsymbol{R} = .218 + .218 = .436$$
$$\boldsymbol{O} = .218 - .218 = 0$$

At the high, therefore, all risk and no opportunity. The two factors, range variability and current price factor, are equal at the high, additive for risk, and they cancel one another for opportunity.

At its low, 46, Monsanto's risk and opportunity are just the reverse:

$$\boldsymbol{R} = .218 - .218 = 0$$
$$\boldsymbol{O} = .218 + .218 = .436$$

All opportunity and no risk.

Note that the RV remained constant at .218 in all of the calculations (indicating a range of 21.8 percent around the average price), but the change in the price between high and low resulted in a range in values for the CPF which varied risk and opportunity between zero and .436.

The Time Element

Strictly speaking, what we have just said about Monsanto's risk and opportunity values at the high and the low must be qualified to take account of changing conditions and the time horizon. In practice, the stock would be tracked continuously, and new projections would be made for the period ahead on the basis of all information available at the time. For example, if Monsanto had touched its high by midyear, and if fundamental data, such as projected earnings, had changed, new risk and opportunity calculations for the period ahead would be based on projected highs and lows during that period.

Comparison with Approach of Modern Capital Market Theorists

It is instructive to apply the approach of the modcaps to the Monsanto figures for the year. Even with the aid of hindsight, they would have measured risk in terms of variability in rate of return, that is, ending price plus dividends minus beginning price, all divided by beginning price:

$$\frac{49\frac{5}{8} - 48\frac{7}{8} + 1.80}{48\frac{7}{8}} = .052$$

This figure alone cannot measure risk by their method. It must be compared with the rate of return for the previous year (or, usually, years). To illustrate, the rate of return for 1971 was .530, so the risk, as measured by mean average deviation, was .250.

They could well get different values by using other measures of variability or by subdividing the years into quarters (as recommended by the Bank Administration Institute) or months (as was done in the SEC's *Institutional Investor Study Report*), but the modcaps would stoutly maintain that throughout any period the price was right, risk was always equal to opportunity, and current price did not alter risk or opportunity at any time.

One can perhaps begin to understand why they've had such a frightful time applying their measures of risk to the investment decision-making process in a dynamic way. They ignore all the action which took place *during* the period selected to measure rate of return.

In contrast, the simple measures we have demonstrated not only separate risk from opportunity, but they also take into account the full ranges in total value, *and* they are able to monitor continuously the dynamic changes which occur in risk and opportunity with change in *current price.*

6

THE RISK/OPPORTUNITY DIAGRAM

As a visual aid to understanding the utilization of the relationship between risk and opportunity, and also in stock selection and portfolio management, it is helpful to plot the values calculated, measuring risk on the vertical axis and opportunity on the horizontal.

Comparing Two Stocks

Figure 6–1 compares two stocks with different volatilities and current prices. The merits of Stock A, with a projected range between 80 and 60, and now selling at 73, can be assessed against Stock B, with a projected range between 85 and 45, and a current price of 54.

Using the formulas developed in the previous chapter, the range variability (RV), or price volatility, of Stock A is only .268 compared to .615 for Stock B. Modern capital market theorists would say that Stock B is more than twice as "risky" as Stock A because B is more than twice as volatile as A. (Variability in rate of return, the modcaps' measure of risk, usually accompanies price volatility.) But this assessment is not true when the current prices are considered. The current price factor (CPF) for Stock A is +.086, whereas that for Stock B is —.277. Combining the two terms for each stock, Stock A has a total risk of .372, higher than the .277 of Stock B. The difference in opportunity values is much greater: .200 for Stock A and .953 for Stock B.

FIGURE 6–1
Risk/Opportunity Diagram Comparing Two Stocks, A and B

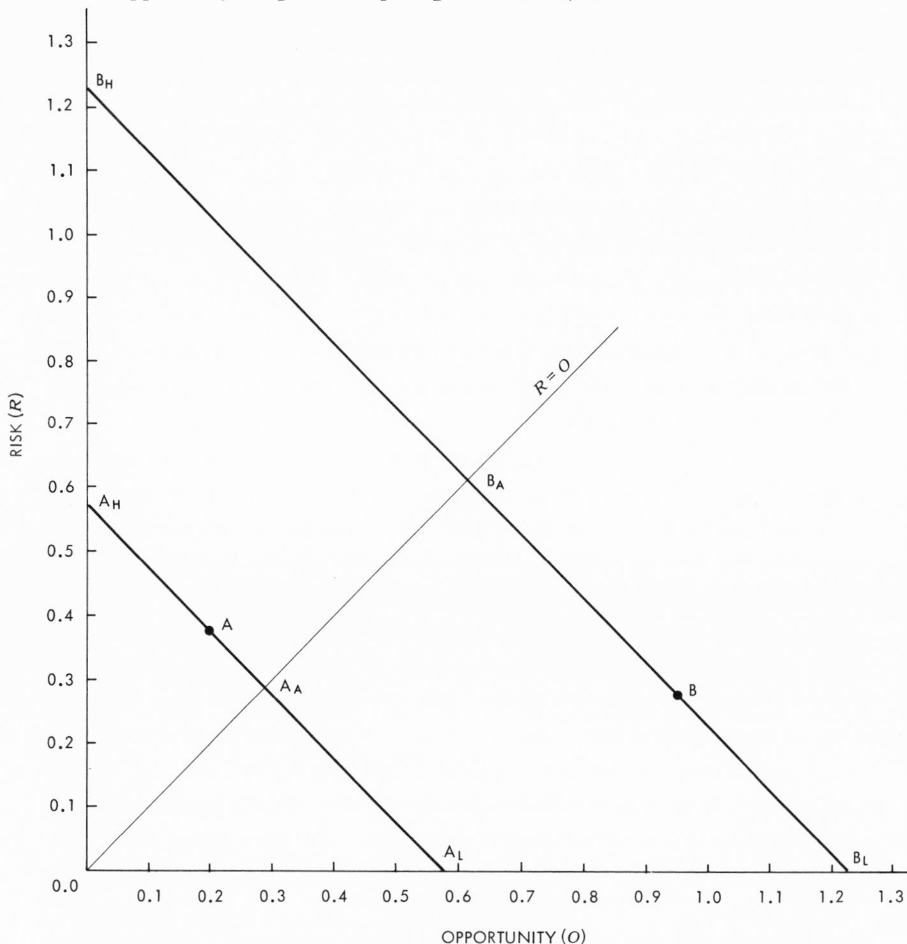

These differences are visually contrasted in Figure 6–1, which clearly indicates the better buy (or hold, or sell) at current prices.

The Volatility Line

The **R/O** (risk/opportunity) diagram is also useful in comparing investment merits as stock prices move over their individual ranges. Stock A, for example, in moving between its high and its low, will traverse the line $A_H A_L$. That line we call the *volatility line* because it is determined by the characteristic, or anticipated, range variability of the individual stock. At point A_A, where current price equals average price, 70, risk and opportunity and range variability are all equal at .286, because the current price factor is zero.

Effect of Current Price

It is only at the intersection of the volatility line and the 45-degree line passing from the origin upwards to the right that risk and opportunity are equal. At all other times, current price is either above or below the average price, and risk is greater or less than opportunity; that is, the stock is either overpriced or underpriced. The current price factor indicates the degree of over- or underpricing at any moment, whatever the price may be.

Stock A at its high (indicated by point A_H) has a risk of .572 (double the RV) and zero opportunity. At the low, 60 (point A_L), risk and opportunity values are reversed.

The same general relationships hold for Stock B, except that values are in line with its greater RV. At point B_A both risk and opportunity equal 0.615; at B_H (price 85) they are 1.230 and zero, respectively; and at B_L (price 45) they are zero and 1.230. It is easily possible, therefore, to compare the merits of these two stocks at all prices between their extremes.

With each stock selling at its average price, the modcaps would be right; B would indeed be more risky than A. But that's only part of the story; at average prices, B would also have a much higher gain potential than A—some 57 percent compared to 14 percent.

One thing to keep in mind when using the risk and opportunity measures is that the denominator for both is average price, not current price, from which possible percentage gains or losses from current price would be calculated.

Using the high, the low, and the starting price, P, of a stock for any particular period, it is a simple matter to calculate (with either hindsight or foresight) the potentials for loss or gain from that starting price. The loss potential, L_P, a measure of risk, is $(P - L)/P$; and the gain potential, G_P, a measure of opportunity, is $(H - P)/P$.

L_P and G_P differ from risk, $\boldsymbol{R}$, and opportunity, $\boldsymbol{O}$, as we measure them because the former are based upon starting price (in the denominator of the equations), while the latter use average price. Although

L_P and G_P are accurate measures of possible losses and gains, it is more advantageous to use the risk and opportunity measures which are related to the average price.

Conceptually, it is useful to separate risk and opportunity into their two component parts, range variability and current price factor. The RV is constant for any given period of time and will often remain a fairly constant characteristic of a stock or portfolio over a long period of time. The CPF, which changes with price, measures just how much a stock is over- or underpriced and is simply added to or subtracted from the more or less constant RV in order to calculate total risk or opportunity.

There is also an advantage when plotting risk and opportunity values, which have finite limits all of which lie on a volatility line running 45 degrees from axis to axis. Changes in current price are reflected in moves of the plotted points along the volatility line that are directly proportional to the price change itself. (See ***R/O*** line, Figure 6–2.)

Although L_P has finite limits (1 when $L = 0$ and 0 when $P = 0$), G_P approaches infinity when P nears zero or H gets very large (it is 0 when $H = P$). The approach to infinity could make plotting difficult in cases where the paper supply is finite. Also, the L_P/G_P lines are not parallel, as are the ***R/O*** volatility lines, but can vary between zero and 90 degrees to either axis, a fact which raises the possibility of a confused picture when several stocks are plotted on the same graph. In addition, price moves are not reflected by proportional moves of plotted points along the L_P/G_P line, as Figure 6–2 illustrates.

When desired, potential gains and losses can either be calculated directly, as were G_P and L_P above, or converted from opportunity and risk measures simply by multiplying by the factor ½(average price/current price); or in percent, 50(average price/current price).

Volatility Classes of Securities

The risk/opportunity diagram also affords a good picture of the relative volatilities of various types of securities and the associated risk and opportunity ranges. The different classes of investment vehicles, as Figure 6–3 shows, range from commodities and warrants down through common stocks and preferreds to convertibles, straight bonds, and Treasury bills, which are very close to cash.

FIGURE 6–2
Risk/Opportunity and Loss Potential/Gain Potential Compared

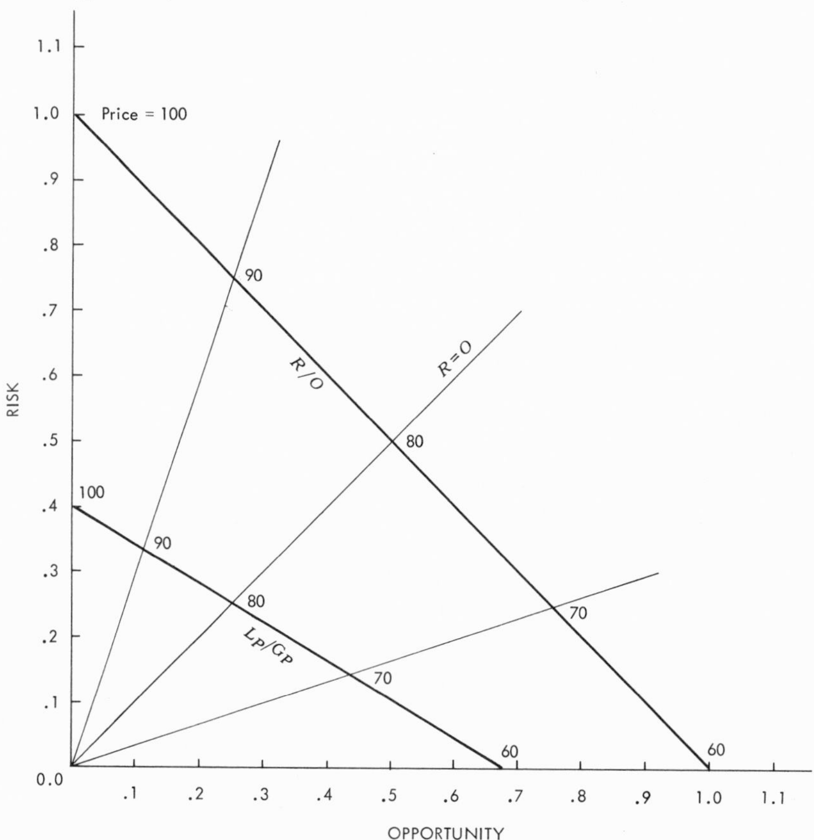

Cash, with no range variability at all, lies at the origin of the diagram. (Try not to think about the effect of inflation on the purchasing power of cash.) The market averages, because of the effect of diversification, lie somewhere near or below low-volatility stocks. (The so-called market-index funds now being pushed by modcaps lie in this same area.) There is, of course, some overlapping of the parallel bands representing each class of security or index. Figure 6–3 indicates only price range variabilities; if fixed income is considered (see next chapter), Treasury bills and some bonds would fall in the negative risk area below the horizontal axis.

The question, "Is a stock riskier than a bond?"—to which the modcaps would answer, "Of course"—can only be answered by calculating

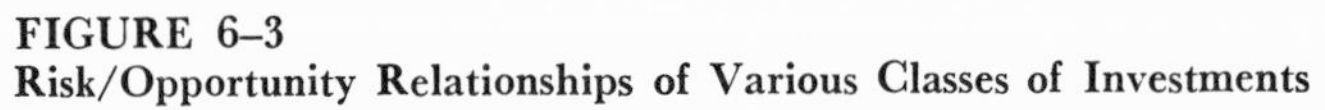

FIGURE 6–3
Risk/Opportunity Relationships of Various Classes of Investments

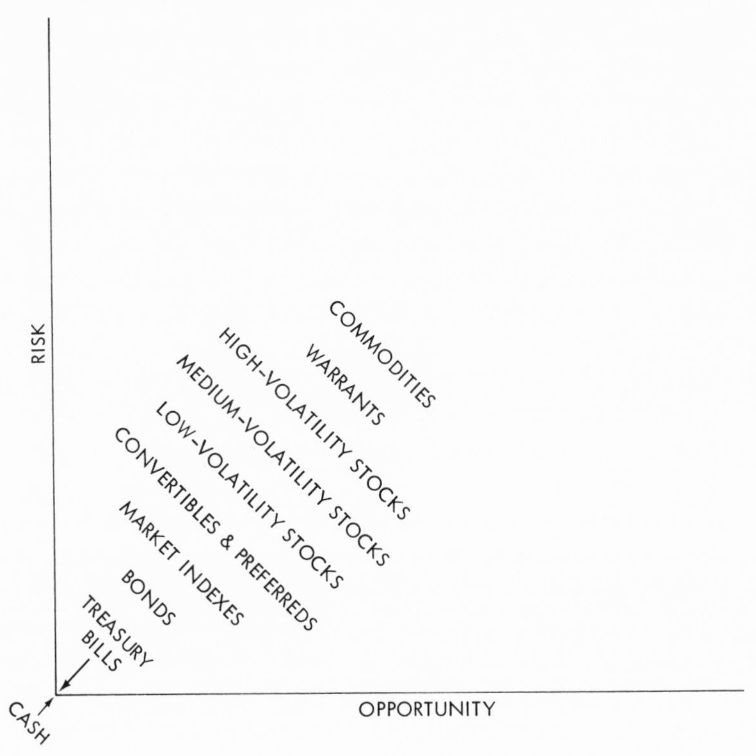

risk on the basis of current prices and range variabilities of the stock and bond in question. The **R/O** diagram may well show that the stock is less risky than the bond. This possibility will come as no surprise to many practitioners, including pension fund managers, many of whom are sitting on bond portfolios whose values have dropped dramatically, as they always do during periods of rapidly rising interest rates. When interest rates decline, of course, there is opportunity for capital appreciation. The **R/O** diagram, coupled with predictions of trends in interest, can provide a good picture of the relative risk and opportunity in bonds—relative to each other and to alternative investment possibilities. (Yield will be considered in Chapter 7.)

The biggest opportunities, however, usually lie in the securities with the highest range variabilities—provided the price is right; that is, if the current price factor is large and favorable.

Uses of the R/O Diagram

The utility of the **R/O** diagram in portfolio management and control (a subject to be treated in more detail later) should be fairly obvious. Besides serving as a device for screening and selection, it can be used for timing buy and sell decisions and for overall control.

Risk, to illustrate, might be controlled by drawing horizontal lines through 0.2 and 0.5, for example. All purchases, then, would be made among securities falling below the 0.2 line, and any security would be sold before it moved across the 0.5 line. Such a policy would permit the holding of low-volatility stocks even when they were "overpriced" but still had some distance to go to reach their highs, while it would dictate selling very high-volatility issues before they even reached their average prices, that is, while they were still "underpriced."

In the same manner, vertical lines could be drawn upward from the opportunity base line, and limits set for purchase and sale.

The other risk and opportunity measures described in Chapter 8 can also be plotted in a similar way and used in conjunction with the **R/O** diagrams.

For large portfolios and for screening large numbers of securities, the **R/O** diagrams must be supplemented by tables, preferably computer printouts, which rank the issues according to opportunity, risk, **O/R** ratio, and so on. We'll expand on this subject later.

7

DIVIDENDS AND INTEREST

THE BASIC FORMULAS for measuring risk and opportunity were derived in Chapter 5. They were based upon price volatility, measured by range variability; and current price, measured by the current price factor. Dividends and other forms of cash income were ignored, because they are usually of only minor importance compared to price changes in determining the profit and loss potentials of most securities, common stocks in particular.

However, dividends and interest can be included in the formulas if more precise values of risk and opportunity are desired; and they should be included in all cases where they amount to an appreciable fraction of the price range of the security in question, as is usually the case with bonds. Moreover, when stocks are being compared with bonds and other fixed income securities on the basis of risk and opportunity, formulas which include the cash income of both should be used.

The formulas which take into account dividends and other cash payments are derived in the same way as the simpler ones of Chapter 5. Because of the cash received, possible loss is decreased by the amount of dividends paid during the period under consideration; and possible gain is increased by the same amount.

The Risk Formula with Dividends

The possible loss is equal to $P - L - D$ (see Figure 7–1). In terms of the basic components, possible loss is equal to $\frac{1}{2}(H - L) - \frac{1}{2}(H + L) - D$. In order to relate these components to the average

FIGURE 7–1
Measuring Risk and Opportunity Based upon Price and Dividends

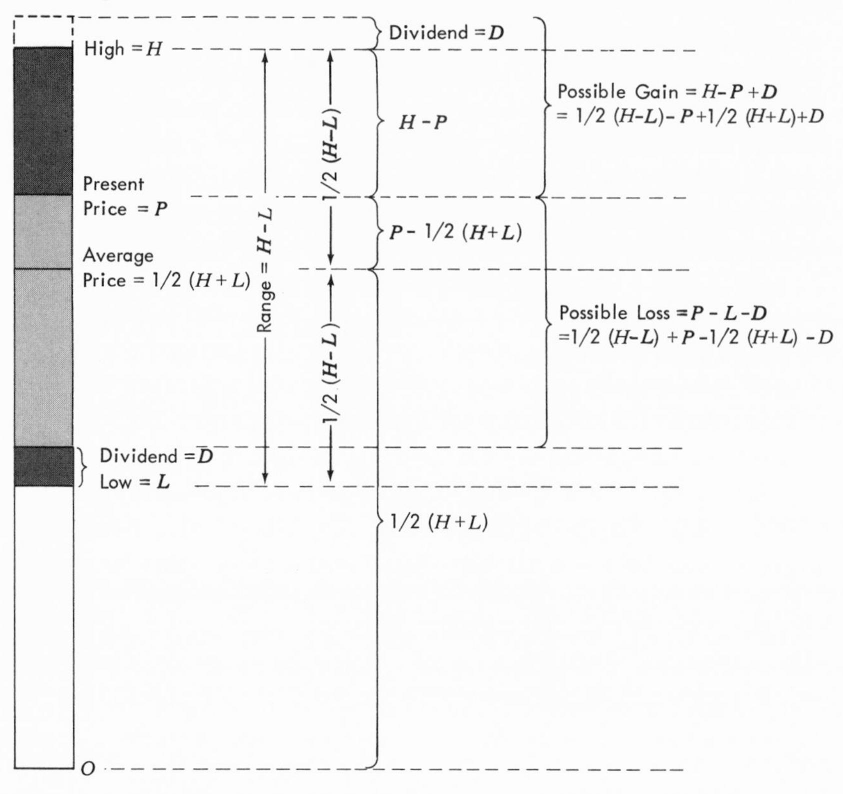

price, we multiply through, as before, by the factor $2/\frac{1}{2}(H + L)$ to obtain the risk measure:

$$\boldsymbol{R} = \frac{H - L}{\frac{1}{2}(H + L)} + 2\,\frac{P - \frac{1}{2}(H + L)}{\frac{1}{2}(H + L)} - \frac{2D}{\frac{1}{2}(H + L)}$$

The first two terms, range variability, RV, and current price factor, CPF, are the same as those in the simpler measure. The third term, called the *dividend factor,* or DF, provides the adjustment for dividends, interest, and other cash payouts.

The Opportunity Formula with Dividends

Similarly, the measure for opportunity is:

$$\boldsymbol{O} = \frac{H - L}{\frac{1}{2}(H + L)} - 2\,\frac{P - \frac{1}{2}(H + L)}{\frac{1}{2}(H + L)} + \frac{2D}{\frac{1}{2}(H + L)}$$

The terms are the same as those in the risk measure, with the algebraic signs reversed for the last two. Dividends decrease risk of loss and increase opportunity for gain.

Using the Measures

To illustrate the use of the measures, we have calculated risk and opportunity values for the common stock, warrants, preferred stock, and three bonds of American Telephone and Telegraph (AT&T) as they would have been at the start of 1972 had highs and lows for the year been predicted accurately.

TABLE 7–1
Risk and Opportunity Measures for Selected Securities of AT&T

Security	*High*	*Low*	*Price*	*D*	*RV*	*CPF**	*DF**	***R***	***O***
Common	53 1/2	41 1/8	44 3/4	2.80	.240	–.108	–.118	.014	.466
Warrant.	9 1/4	5 1/2	8 3/4	.00	.508	+.373	.000	.881	.135
$4 Prefrd. . . .	62 5/8	57	59 1/4	4.00	.094	–.019	–.134	–.059	.247
7.75s 77	107 7/8	104 1/2	107	7.75	.032	+.015	–.146	–.099	.163
7s 2001.	99 7/8	94 1/8	99 1/4	7.00	.059	+.046	–.144	–.039	.157
2 7/8s 87.	64	60	61 1/2	2.875	.065	–.016	–.093	–.044	.174

*Algebraic signs are for risk; they are reversed to calculate opportunity.
Note: Highs and lows are for 1972. Price is on 12/31/71.

Table 7–1 shows that the common stock, with the highest opportunity and very little risk, would have been the best buy for most investors seeking high return with low risk. Both the current price factor and the dividend factor diminished risk and increased opportunity.

The warrant was much more risky than the stock (.881 versus .014), both on the basis of volatility and current price, and of course warrants pay no dividends to diminish risk. This is the type of security, with high risk as measured by high variability in rate of return (which normally accompanies high price volatility), that the modern capital market theorists believe will, on average, deliver the highest return. The modcaps, of course, always ignore current price, even when, as in this case, the relatively high current price increases risk and decreases opportunity. The warrant was, in fact, the very worst choice that AT&T could offer investors at that moment in time.

The $4 preferred stock and the three bonds all had negative risk, meaning that the income in each case more than covered any possible loss due to a drop in price. All four securities approached the class of those which, like Treasury bills, are considered to offer a risk-free rate of return. The former, however, are not quite so risk free, because price change makes the rate of return more uncertain, even though it is positive.

The preferred stock had a higher opportunity rating than any of the bonds, and even less risk than the 7s of 2001 and the 2⅞s of 1987—a good, safe buy for the conservative investor.

Of the three bonds, the 7.75s of 1977, with the lowest risk and only slightly less opportunity than the 2⅞s, seem to be the best buy for the year ahead, even though they were selling for a premium at the start. For the longer term, of course, such factors as premiums and discounts and bond ratings enter into the bond investment decision process.

The common stock of AT&T is a good example of the relative importance of dividends in assessing risk and opportunity in so-called blue chip stocks, which often pay dividends in the 5 percent area and exhibit low price volatility compared to most other stocks. As Table 7–1 shows, the dividend factor has only about one half the weight of the range variability, although the DF was slightly greater than the CPF at the start of the period. During the year, however, the current price factor varied between +.240 and −.240, each extreme almost more than double the magnitude of the dividend factor.

Relative Importance of Dividends and Price Change

AT&T's gain potential between its low and its high was 30.1 percent compared to a dividend yield of 6.3 percent on the price of the stock at the start of the year. Furthermore, the swing between low and high took place in approximately six months, meaning that the gain potential from price change, when annualized, was about 60 percent, nearly 10 times the dividend rate.

So we see once again that the potential for gain (and loss) through investment in common stocks lies predominantly in the magnitude and frequency of price changes. If this statement applies to a stodgy stock like AT&T, it goes double, and often much more than double, for high-flying institutional darlings like Burroughs, Polaroid, and Xerox.

Naturally, taking advantage of price swings is a much more difficult matter than buying and holding a stock with a dependable dividend record. Very few money managers, in fact, have demonstrated the talent consistently, although many have tried. The general lack of success has given a bad name to "trading" (as opposed to "investing"). But even buy-and-hold types, to be successful, must buy in at favorable prices and eventually get out at favorable prices.

A possible exception to this general rule may seem to lie in the current concentration of major institutional fund managers on a score of stocks like IBM, Xerox, Philip Morris, Eastman Kodak, Polaroid, and Avon Products. This concentration has driven many price-earnings ratios out of sight, but the high prices based upon such demand have been self-fulfilling; rising prices make everyone's portfolio performance look good, so why try to take profits and spoil the game?

In the long run, nevertheless, the acid test of the portfolio manager is how he handles price changes—not how much dividend income he can claim credit for. This will even prove true, we predict, for the currently popular bond funds. That the biggest *opportunities* for capital appreciation lie in fairly short-term price changes (say 3 to 12 months) can hardly be denied, even when taxes must be considered for positions held for less than 6 months. The richer-than-Croesus pension funds, of course, need not worry about taxes.

The general failure to capitalize on shorter term price changes can be accounted for, not by some version of the random-walk theory, but by the fact that no reliable method has been available for determining when stocks are underpriced or overpriced, and for measuring how much.

This basic need can be fulfilled to a large extent by the risk and opportunity measures we have demonstrated. Success in their use will still depend not only upon accurate estimation of highs and lows but also upon selection and timing. All of these matters require great skill, and even the most skillful cannot expect to buy at the lows and sell at the highs all the time. But the point is this: even partial success can be extremely rewarding. Even capturing only *half* the gain potential of stodgy AT&T in 1972 would have meant a gain of 15 percent in six months or less—a record any fund manager could boast about. Plus dividends, naturally.

Definitions

The inclusion of a dividend factor in the equations measuring risk and opportunity calls for slight modifications in the basic definitions.

Risk is exposure to the possibility of loss resulting from a drop in price, lessened by the amount of dividends received.

Opportunity is exposure to the possibility of gain resulting from a rise in price, increased by the amount of dividends received.

8

MORE MEASURES OF RISK AND OPPORTUNITY

ADDITIONAL MEASURES of risk and opportunity, both absolute and relative to the market as a whole, can be developed quite simply from the basic measures already demonstrated.

Basic Measures

To summarize and illustrate the basic measures: *Range variability,* a measure of *price volatility,* is the difference between the high price and the low, divided by the average price. IBM, which rose to a high of 426¾ during the past year and touched a low of 331¾, thus had a range variability, RV, of .250; that is, its price fluctuated 25 percent around its average. IBM's more volatile competitor, Burroughs, with a high of 229½ and a low of 146, had an RV of .445, indicating a price fluctuation of 44.5 percent around its average.

For comparison, the theoretical maximum fluctuation for any stock is 200 percent; that is, 100 percent above its average and 100 percent below (down to zero). Although certain stocks in the news as this is written seem to be probing the lower limit (Equity Funding comes to mind, along with Presidential Reassurance), it is a rare stock which even approaches an RV of 2, the theoretical upper limit, and almost all stay well below 1. (The lower limit, for cash, say, is zero.) During 1972 the relatively hot institutional favorite Philip Morris had an RV of .543 and Polaroid's, at .538, was almost as volatile. Xerox was only .351 and Avon, .391. General Motors, even tamer than AT&T (.220), was only .173.

These volatility figures, even by themselves, are of some help in the search for big winners, because potential gain can go hand in hand with volatility, provided the price is right.

The *current price factor,* CPF, tells whether a stock is under- or overpriced at any given moment and by how much. It is based simply upon whether a stock is selling below or above its average price, and this is calculated by subtracting the average price from the current price, dividing by the average price, and multiplying by 2. Why 2? So that the CPF will be equal to the RV at both the high and the low and satisfy the mathematical requirement that opportunity and risk (see below) be equal to zero at the high and the low respectively. (The basic formulas were derived in Chapter 5.) The theoretical limits for the CPF are +2 and −2, but in practice the figures are even smaller than the RV's mentioned above (except at the high and the low, when they are equal). As current price approaches average price, the CPF approaches zero.

To illustrate with three of the examples used above, IBM, selling at 336½ at the start of the period, has a CPF of −.225; Burroughs, selling at 152¾, was even more underpriced, with a CPF of −.373. General Motors, one of the few institutional favorites overpriced at the time, had a CPF of +.064.

Risk, defined as exposure to the possibility of loss due to a drop in price, is the comprehensive measure that results from combining range variability with the current price factor. For IBM, risk, $\mathbf{R} = .250 - .225 = .025$; for Burroughs, $\mathbf{R} = .445 - .373 = .072$. Both are selling well below their average prices, so that their negative CPF's almost eliminate the risk stemming from volatility. The measures show, however, that Burroughs is somewhat more risky.

The counterpart of risk, *opportunity,* defined as exposure to the possibility of gain due to a rise in price, also combines RV and CPF, but with a reversal in algebraic sign. In other words, although volatility contributes positively and equally to risk and opportunity, a current price below average means reduced risk and increased opportunity, while a current price above average means increased risk and reduced opportunity. For example, for IBM, opportunity, $\mathbf{O} = .250 + .225 = .475$; for Burroughs, $\mathbf{O} = .445 + .373 = .818$, a much higher figure than IBM's, indicating a much greater appreciation potential.

The theoretical limits for both risk and opportunity are zero and 4, but it is a rare stock that rises much above 1, because most RV's are .5 or below and CPF's even smaller. However, at the start of 1972, Philip Morris had an opportunity of 1.032; Polaroid, 1.027.

The *dividend factor,* used to adjust the basic risk and opportunity measures, was demonstrated in Chapter 7. It should be used in those cases where dividends, interest, and other cash payouts appreciably affect the accuracy of the measures derived from price alone. This factor, which varies from zero up to some indefinite positive figure, depending upon the amount of the dividend and the price of the stock, is not considered in the theoretical limits of the other measures described in this chapter, which are based solely upon prices.

Opportunity/Risk Ratio

Having calculated risk and opportunity, it can be useful to determine their ratios in order to see what a unit of opportunity, say, is worth in terms of risk—or vice versa. For IBM, the **O/R** ratio is 19.0 compared to Burrough's 11.4. Because the **O/R** ratios approach infinity as risk approaches zero, their comparability is less meaningful in the upper reaches. Around 5, say, and under, they can be very useful in screening and selection, but they should always be considered in the light of the simple risk and opportunity figures themselves. For example, although IBM's **O/R** ratio exceeds that of Burroughs, both have very low risk, so the much higher appreciation potential of Burroughs would point to it as the better buy for an alert portfolio manager at the start of 1972.

The inverse of the **O/R** ratio, the **R/O** or risk/opportunity ratio, can be useful in emphasizing the number of units of risk necessary to capture one unit of opportunity.

The absolute measures demonstrated above were illustrated with only a very few stocks. The utility of the measures, as one would expect, increases with the number of stocks to be screened and selected during the investment decision-making process. For a limited number of securities, a graphical display like the one shown in Chapter 6 is very helpful. For larger numbers, computer printouts showing not only values but rankings are essential.

All of these measures, of course, can be applied to entire portfolios, such as those of mutual and pension funds, as well as to individual securities and all kinds of market indexes.

Market-Related Measures

Absolute measures of risk and opportunity, when applied to some general index such as the Dow Jones Industrials (DJI) or the New York Stock Exchange (NYSE) composite average, can be used to assess whether or not the "market" itself is "overpriced" or "underpriced," and by how much. Just as with individual stocks, market highs and lows must be forecast—through the use of economic indicators, price/earnings ratios, or whatever method of divination the analyst finds effective.

We usually prefer working with the NYSE composite, and, with our own crystal ball, we managed to come quite close to the actual figures for 1972. Even better, however, was 20/20 hindsight, which showed a low of 56.23 near the start of the year and a high of 65.48 near its end. The market, in other words, was almost all up from the 1971 close at 56.43. At the start, therefore, the market, as represented by the composite index, was almost all opportunity (.298) and almost no risk (.006), based on range variability of .152 and a current price factor of —.146. Comparable figures for the DJI: RV = .153, CPF = —.151, **R** = .002, **O** = .304.

Comparative measures of risk and opportunity are obtained simply by dividing the figures for a security or portfolio by the corresponding figures for the selected index. These comparative measures are useful in assessing the characteristics of a stock or portfolio against the market as a standard.

The beta coefficient of the modern capital market theorists is a measure of market-related variability in rate of return. A perfectly diversified portfolio, say the modcaps, has the same beta as the market, and higher returns than the market's can be achieved only by assuming higher risk.

What we have called, in a *Barron's* article,[62] the *Poor Boy beta* is based upon price variability instead of what the modcaps call, not very realistically, rate of return. Our Poor Boy beta, perhaps better and more precisely termed *range variability/market ratio,* is simply the ratio of the range variability of a stock or portfolio (RV_S) to that of the market (RV_M).

For IBM, RV_S/RV_M = .250/.152 = 1.645, meaning that the price of IBM stock moves up or down, on average, 1.645 percent for every 1 percent move of the NYSE composite index. In other words, IBM is over 64 percent more volatile than the market. For Burroughs, RV_S/RV_M = .445/.152 = 2.928. Even AT&T, during 1972, at least, was more volatile than the market: RV_S/RV_M = .262/.152 = 1.724. Telephone was, in fact, more volatile than IBM during the period; this is just the opposite of what one would expect from the modcaps' beta ratings, based upon historical data covering, commonly, the past five years. (Valve Line's beta is .50 for Telephone, .88 for IBM.)

The above example (and many more could be cited) lends emphasis to the fact that the business of portfolio management cannot be run solely on the basis of volatility numbers or averages. The greatest opportunities, in fact, lie in anomalies and disequilibrium.

A good measure of current disequilibrium is the current price factor, which measures how much a stock is under- or overpriced. The stock's CPF can be compared to that of the market (when algebraic signs are the same) by the *current price factor/market ratio.* To illustrate, for IBM, CPF_S/CPF_M = —.225/—.146. = 1.541; and for Burroughs CPF_S/CPF_M = —.373/—.146 = 2.555. When the signs are opposite, the algebraic difference can be used to indicate the degree of over- or underpricing relative to the market.

Probably the most useful of the relative measures is the *opportunity/market ratio,* which compares the opportunity of a stock or portfolio to that of the market as a whole. For IBM, $\boldsymbol{O}_S/\boldsymbol{O}_M$ = .475/.298 = 1.594, which in spite of its lower volatility made it seem like a better buy than AT&T, $\boldsymbol{O}_S/\boldsymbol{O}_M$ = .370/.298 = 1.242, but not as good as Burroughs, $\boldsymbol{O}_S/\boldsymbol{O}_M$ = .818/.298 = 2.745, which had nearly three times the gain potential of the market.

In the same fashion, the *risk/market ratio,* $\mathbf{R}_S/\mathbf{R}_M$, can be used to assess the risk of a security or portfolio in relation to that of the market. In our risk article in *Barron's,* adhering to the Greek tradition, we termed this the *kappa coefficient* (because, we guess, it korrects both stock and market risk for kurrent price).

The relative measures described above are best used in conjunction with the absolute measures upon which they are based. *Relative rankings* between stocks—for example, for risk—are the same for both absolute and relative measures; the latter add a useful comparison with the overall market.

9

THE GOOD NEWS AND THE BAD NEWS

In the earlier chapters we indicated with several examples how measures of risk and opportunity can be used to assess the investment value of securities at any moment in time. Now, before we demonstrate how these measures can be used to enhance and control all of the vital steps in a logical program of portfolio management, let's look at (1) what the measures cannot do; (2) what the measures can do for every investor; and, in the following chapters, (3) how to determine and use the two unknowns in the formulas, the highs and the lows.

The Caveat

First the caveat: although the measures themselves are simple, skill is still required in their application, in determining the proper highs and lows, and in timing. The plain truth is that if this approach is adopted on a wide scale, only a very small minority will apply it consistently with great success. This is as it should be. No system, however good it may be, will work for long if everyone is doing the same thing.

Especially in the stock market, the competent, to be successful, must have incompetents to trade with. Luckily for the competent few, there is no danger that the supply of incompetents will dry up, for they are to be found among professional pension fund trustees and mutual fund managers as surely as among the individual investors they may disdainfully call the public or the little guy. In fact, statistical studies have shown that the institutional investors whose records are most easily checked—the managers of mutual funds—have on average failed to perform even as well as the market indexes or a portfolio selected at random; and no proof is available to show that the managers of mutual funds are any worse than other run-of-the-mill professional money managers. This would seem to indicate that the public, since someone must be doing *better* than the averages, is having greater success than the pros. (Or are the floor specialists taking up all the slack?)

The trouble with statistical studies is that they tend to boil down all their figures to averages and then to draw their conclusions in terms of generalities, ignoring or explaining away the anomalies—which may actually hold more significance than the averages. We believe that competence is to be found among various classes of investors, but that it is a rare quality. The ability to excel—almost by definition—is found only in the few. That statement is just as true of the stock market as it is of any other arena of human endeavor. Mutual funds, for example, are bound to show about the same average performance as the market itself, because the sample studied is such a large part of the market (and they're bound to do worse, on average, as some studies have shown, if transaction and other costs are considered).

The stock market—in spite of the dogma of modern capital market theorists—is not a random walk over practical investment time periods; it does not follow the same physical laws that govern Brownian motion; only the generally low level of competence makes it seem that way. Yet the same modcaps argue that the thing which assures the efficiency of the market is the participation and interaction of many highly skilled professional money managers. Today, with many of the little guys driven away from the market (mainly by inequitable brokerage fees), most of the trading is being done by the professionals. Is the market now more efficient? Just the opposite; price changes are more erratic than they ever were.

Quantification vs. Emotion

We've delivered the bad news that only a few can excel; now for the good news. Anyone can play and many can win. Anyone, no matter what his present level of competence or incompetence may be, can *improve* his investment performance by applying the quantitative approach developed here. One need not come in first to win at the investment game; one must merely avoid losing.

Any systematic approach that gives the investor an edge over the competition improves his chances of winning. The quantitative method—even if all it does is to distill an investor's information and misinformation, hopes and fears, into numbers—gives him an advantage over the generally emotional and often hysterical competition.

For example, if he can say to himself, "Well, the market took another beating today, and I admit I'm scared. All of my friends and even my broker are bailing out, even if it means taking big losses. And yet, my portfolio numbers look better than ever: opportunity 0.8, risk 0.1; seems like good odds on any deal, and the opportunity-to-market ratio is about 3. Economic news is good, earnings are up. What do I have to worry about? In fact, instead of giving way to panic like the others, I may buy something I've been tracking that's ridiculously underpriced at these levels, namely . . . ."

Indeed, the market may drop still lower—and probably will—but the numbers can give assurance to the investor that a turnaround is likely and also give him the courage to take advantage unemotionally of the best buying opportunities. Emotional selling is greatest at market bottoms.

Emotional tensions are reversed during market booms. Now all of Our Hero's friends are buying Pizzatronics, Pat-A-Kake Franchise Systems, and Zuccini-Lox Leasing, which are hitting new highs almost daily. His broker advises sagely that you can't argue with success. And he has a friend who teaches at the business school who tells him that it's an efficient market, prices are always where they should be, and the riskier stocks—on average, of course—give the highest return if only one demands it. So the investor looks again at his numbers. He has already liquidated some of his boomers on the way up as they moved into high-risk/low-opportunity areas. But, caught up in the excitement of the bull market, and not wishing to ignore the hot deals his friends are chasing, he assesses the risk/opportunity ratios of Pizzatronics et al., finds them excessive—and sells short.

An unreachable ideal? Of course! It's Kipling's "Iffy" character transferred to the stock market: "If you can keep your head when all about you are losing theirs . . . ." But although the ideal may be unreachable, it is not unapproachable. Our objective, remember, is not necessarily to come in first, but to come out ahead.

We mentioned earlier the possibility of including misinformation in the quantification process. This will, of course, decrease the odds on success; but the quantification of even one material fact—as opposed to an emotional reaction to it—will increase the odds on profitable application of the method. The degree to which the ideal is realizable is proportional to the relevance and accuracy of the data quantified, naturally.

In sum, the quantification of risk and opportunity can help any portfolio manager improve his performance and best his competitors in the marketplace. Those who apply the method with the greatest skill—and they must, in the nature of things, be few—will come out at the very top; others must be content with a reasonable level of solvency.

Adam Smith Was Right

Not the least of the advantages stemming from the quantification of risk and opportunity is the beneficial psychological effect it can have on the investor. In all the history of investment, no one ever bought a stock, option, or tulip bulb believing that its price would subsequently go down.

"The chance of gain is by every man more or less over-valued, and the chance of loss is by most men under-valued," wrote Adam Smith in *The Wealth of Nations.* "The over-weening conceit which the greater part of men have of their own abilities, is an ancient evil remarked by the philosophers and moralists of all ages. Their absurd presumption of their own good fortune, has been less taken notice of. It is, however, if possible, still more universal."

Although ill fortune seems never to be anticipated, history shows clearly that prices go down as well as up. When the dreadful event occurs, investors react with unreasoning surprise and anguish. The phenomenon is not restricted to amateurs; the floor of the New York Stock Exchange is a dreary place when prices are dropping, and murmurs of concern for pension fund assets (and trustees' jobs) are heard in the paneled quarters of bank trust departments.

The formulas for assessing risk and opportunity have no magical powers, regrettably, to prevent prices from dropping. What they do, however, is force the investor to consider in advance the *possibility* of a price drop and to project a low price as well as a high one. The resultant measures may rule out a purchase if the risk is too high at that point, or they may indicate a wait for a more favorable purchase price—but even with the help of the formulas one cannot hope to buy in, except by chance, at the projected low, which may never be reached. It is quite enough to buy when opportunity is high and risk low.

Let's say our investor foresees a good earnings gain for IBM and a hefty price increase, to 420 if all goes well. In spite of his enthusiasm, he is forced to consider what might happen under less favorable circumstances, and after weighing volatility and other relevant factors, estimates a possible low of 320. Current price is 337. With range variability of .270 and current price factor of —.178, risk is only .092 and opportunity a solid .448, an **O/R** ratio near 5.

He buys at 337, rather than waiting for the low, because he feels that the stock will take off fast in a bull market. IBM drops 5 points, to 332. Does he despair, like the ordinary investor? Of course—but only momentarily. He has already decided that he can live with a low of 320, and 335 is still well above that figure. He even consoles himself with the thought that as price drops, risk gets lower and opportunity greater; Our Hero even decides that he may buy some more IBM if the price drops down near his projected low. It does not; IBM bottoms at 331¾ and then climbs to a high of 426¾ before easing off for the rest of the year. (The figures are for 1972.)

Anyone, but Anyone, Can Play

Another advantage to the quantitative approach whose only unknowns are projected high and low prices within the selected time horizon is that anyone can play, from the most dedicated fundamentalist to the most wild-eyed seer.

Fundamentalists

The strictest fundamentalists, following Benjamin Graham and David L. Dodd, are forever seeking "intrinsic value" or "central value" as a measure of what the price *should* be. This approach is a sound one and tends to pay off in the long run. Its major weakness is that it tends to exclude the real growth stocks which, by the time they are discovered, always have price/earnings ratios so high that the price is higher than the intrinsic value at which fundamentalists would take a position. Thus, the fundamentalists miss out on stocks like IBM, Polaroid, and Xerox.

If all fundamental data were applied to forecasting highs and lows rather than in trying to pinpoint intrinsic value at some point in time, the fundamentalists' task would be simplified, because it is easier to forecast a price range during some selected time period than to determine the right price on a certain date. The central value toward which all prices tend to return may well be intrinsic value—and indeed it could be substituted for average value in the formulas—but the mean between the high and low is a simpler and more practical measure of central tendency, particularly for the shorter term. Stock prices have many times demonstrated their ability to stay clear of intrinsic value for years on end.

Graham and Dodd also mention "anticipated market value" and "relative value" as the other two basic approaches to stock valuation but hold them in less esteem than intrinsic value. All three methods can use the risk and opportunity measures.

Theorists

Related to the fundamentalists are the theorists who believe, with considerable justification, that the true value of a stock is the present value of the future stream of dividends (or earnings; they say it makes no difference) discounted at some suitable rate of interest. This, too, could be used as the measure of central tendency in the formulas, instead of the algebraic mean. As with intrinsic value, however, some complications can arise in cases where these values fall outside the high-low range.

A probabilistic approach can also be employed to determine "expected price," and the resultant figure used as the measure of central tendency. By this method, the range is divided into equal segments, each of which is weighted according to its probability of occurrence (the sum of the weights being equal to one), and the sum of the products is divided by the number of segments. To illustrate, if the range is expected to be between 60 and 100, and the probabilities of the higher prices are judged to be greater than those of the low, the expected value would be greater than the algebraic mean, 80—perhaps something like 85 or 90, depending upon the weights assigned. The result might well be more accurate, but in view of the much greater effort involved, and also of the fact that the weights assigned are largely subjective estimates in any case, most analysts would probably be content to settle for the simple average.

Chartists

So-called technical analysts, mainly "chartists," fall in another group who should appreciate risk and opportunity measures based upon highs and lows, for terms like *support level, resistance level, measured move* and *channel* have a prominent place in their pseudotechnical jargon.

It takes a trained eye, to say the least, to identify and interpret some of their "formations." One reason we call their approach pseudotechnical is that the variety of interpretations is limited only by the number of chartists. (*Real* technicians, in contrast, come up with about the same answers.) The random-walk theorists say that technical analysis is utter nonsense, that past price patterns are no clue to the future, or as George 'Adam Smith' Goodman put it in *The Money Game,* "the market has no memory." However, people make the market, and they do have memories.

We're willing to go along with the chartists in their belief in trends (another source of hilarity among the random walkers). Some stocks do, in fact, exhibit persistent trends which can last for a period of years, because they are soundly based on such fundamentals as the trend in earnings. In projecting highs and lows, it makes sense (and violates no natural law) to go along with the trend if no major change in the fundamentals is anticipated.

By saying this, we do not mean to endorse "technical analysis." Quite the opposite. Except for their concepts of trends and the effect of supply and demand on stock prices, we would favor the heave-ho for the whole anthropomorphic monster—head, shoulders, and double bottom. Of course, charts (as opposed to "chartists" who use them to predict the future) can serve many useful purposes.

In fact, we should thank the statisticians whose studies have exposed the ineffectiveness of this sort of technical legerdemain. They have been just as hard on the fundamentalists, of course, and not without reason, for the present state of the art leaves much to be desired. However, that's not the reason the modcaps cite; they attribute the poor performance of professional analysts as well as fund managers to a kind of natural law—that of the efficient market, sired by the random-walk theory, out of Brownian motion.

Why Don't the Pros Do Better?

Actually, it is not fair to attribute poor performance to any failure of the *concept* of fundamental analysis. The blame really lies with the general low state of the art, and often, we suspect, with the rejection of much analysis by money managers.

Just what sort of fundamental analysis was applied to Equity Funding, for example, before that scandal broke, revealing that the company's splendid "growth" record was based upon fictional policies dreamed up by its insurance subsidiary? *Business Week* was moved to editorialize:

> Inevitably, several dozen banks, accounting firms, regulatory agencies, and investment managers are going to come out looking lazy, or stupid, or both. The irony is that if any one of them had asked a few intelligent, skeptical questions, the whole scheme would have been exposed in the early stages.
>
> . . . the portfolio managers who were so enchanted by finding a razzle-dazzle growth stock should have taken a harder look at the nature of that growth before they rushed to buy a piece of it.
>
> . . . there is a difference between trust and sheer gullibility. Apparently the victims in the Equity Funding case did not grasp the distinction.[11]

Among the notable victims were many of the nation's largest banks, particularly Morgan Guaranty and Bankers Trust, those with the biggest trust departments, which, as the article accompanying the *Business Week* editorial pointed out, are not obliged to disclose stock ownership, as are mutual funds for example. New York's First National City Bank, along with other generous lenders, gave more than $50 million to Equity Funding in the form of loans.

Institutional victims with the largest holdings of Equity Funding stock just before the bubble burst (and in many cases afterwards, as well) included two affiliates of Boston Company (John W. Bristol and Institutional Investors), Fidelity Corporation of Virginia, and Ohio State Teachers Pension Fund. *The Wall Street Journal* reported that Institutional Investors sold over 400,000 shares while its fellow Boston Company unit was buying.

Although Equity Funding had been following its crooked path for more than ten years, happily conjuring up fake policyholders and selling them to reinsurers (other insurance companies run by less imaginative men), brokers were high on the stock right up to the final curtain. *Business Week*[13] quotes words of praise from Smith, Barney, Wertheim & Company and Burnham & Company. Even Standard & Poor's, which turns out reams of data and research material to guide investors of all stripes, joined in the general approbation.

Still other prominent institutional investors and financial organizations which invested in, or recommended purchase of, Equity Funding included, according to the *Journal,* Fiduciary Trust Company of New York, the Ford Foundation, Loews Corporation, Chemical Bank of New York, Hayden Stone, Inc., Oppenheimer & Company, and even one of the smartest Wall Street hedge funds, Steinhardt, Fine, Berkowitz.

Now the lawyers have gotten into the act, so we can be sure that the farce has a long time to run. The point we wish to make here is that every one of the big, reputable, financial institutions mentioned—banks, brokers, insurance companies—supports a highly paid research department, supposedly giving some consideration to the fundamentals, and yet they were all gulled!

The Equity Funding case, along with those of Penn Central, Four Seasons Nursing, and other spectacular flops, gives dramatic proof that the fundamental approach to stock evaluation—even though it is the only logical one—still has a long way to go, both in the development of its methods and in its acceptance by money managers. Many of the latter, incidentally, are reported to have huddled frequently with Equity Funding's president, Stanley Goldblum, to receive his personal assurances that the marvelous growth would continue. Personal assessment of the quality of management is rated high by most money managers.

Even after dark rumors about the company had circulated in Wall

Street for some time, many fund managers and analysts, presumably after checking their fundamentals and finding them sound, still favored the stock. Finally, the man who blew the whistle on Equity Funding—Raymond L. Dirks, "a widely known analyst of insurance stocks," said the *Journal*—started calling his clients with the bad news, based on a telephone call from a disgruntled ex-employee, not on his previous analysis of fundamentals.

Perhaps fundamental analysis should begin routinely with the question, "Is the president crooked?" If this question cannot be answered by looking at or listening to him for a few moments (in a surprising number of cases it can be), then a closely related question can often be answered by examination of the annual report: "Does the president encourage or condone crooked or misleading accounting?" We have another question, which may not find favor with all readers: "Is the president a lawyer and, if so, why?"

We may be tempted to think of spectacular failures like Equity Funding, National Student Marketing, and others as glaring but isolated cases. However, precisely because they were so glaring, their weaknesses should have been that much easier to detect. The conclusion is inescapable that the assessment process is badly flawed.

Even though fundamental analysis is the only approach based upon logic and is, we firmly believe, the only one that can lead to superior performance, it must be admitted that it has so far failed to prove its superiority over such alternatives as chart reading or, for that matter, the reading of tea leaves or entrails.

A Selection of Seers

An astrologer appears regularly on the financial television station in Los Angeles to analyze the fortunes of companies and their stocks. The idea may seem utterly silly to most serious investors, but evidently there is a continuing demand for his services, and who can say that the results obtained by his followers are any worse than those obtained by adherents of the alternate methods now available?

Only today (as this is written) *The Wall Street Journal*[71] carried a story about the SEC's charges of fraud against an investment advisory firm called Advanced Analysis, Inc., headed by Stuart A. Schwalbe. Just how advanced it is may be judged by the fact that Mr. Schwalbe claims he can predict "upside and downside movements of individual securities" through the use of extrasensory perception. The SEC charges, we note, are not based upon any objective assessment of the utility of the ESP approach, but rather upon what it considered excessive and unproved claims by the seer, and specifically upon nondisclosure of an old two-month suspension by the NYSE, and because he recently represented that his abilities had been "passed upon" by the commission.

Another approach to stock valuation, perhaps aptly termed the "play-it-by-ear" school, is represented by a broker who told Dan Dorfman, of *The Wall Street Journal,* why he was bearish and taking short positions in Pickwick International, a tape and record concern which had racked up 79 consecutive quarters of rising earnings over year-earlier periods. The broker admitted that he had never even talked to management and was not "overly familiar with the company business," but that "he hadn't heard any new musical sounds that excited him; thus he thought there could be a slowing of growth in the record business." The clincher, for him, was the SEC's reports on insider transactions, which showed that most of the company's officers and directors were selling their stock."

"I'm not suggesting anything wrong," the broker said. "But it does make you wonder. And if I'm wrong? C'est la vie; you win a few, you lose a few."[19]

As we said, anyone can play. But quantification may come a bit harder for some than for others.

Summary

To sum up the good news and the bad news: Everyone can play; many can win; only a few can excel.

10

PREDICTING HIGHS AND LOWS

IN ORDER TO MEASURE risk and opportunity only three numbers are necessary: the high, the low, and the current price. All of these are readily available for past time periods of any selected duration, and there are many valid reasons for making calculations based on 20/20 hindsight—for example, to assess performance in the light of the risk taken or the opportunity missed.

Much more useful, obviously, and much more difficult, is the process of estimating risk and opportunity for future time periods. Because current price is always known, only two figures—the high and the low—need be forecast. This fact may make the task seem easier than it really is.

Simple price projections can, of course, be based upon nothing more complicated than price trends, and risk and opportunity calculations based on such projections will prove useful if the trends persist, as they often do. However, the greatest success will be achieved by those who are best able to distill all relevant information into accurate predictions of highs and lows. As we indicated earlier, the method can help any investor outperform those with the same information who do not quantify the data at their disposal. And also (to repeat the caveat), only a relative few, by definition, will excel, that is, show consistent performance over time in the topmost ranks. The corollary is that the reader will have his own work cut out for him. Our responsibility, we think, is to supply superior tools and method of operation.

Time Horizon

The first step to be taken in estimating highs and lows is to decide on one factor which is not even one of the specific variables in the formula, but which nevertheless determines them. That factor is the time period during which the highs and lows will occur. In general, the longer the time period, the greater the range between high and low.

The time period selected will depend in part on the time horizon of the individual or institutional investor, which can vary from that of the short-term trader to that of the buy-and-hold trust fund—from a month or less up to several years—and it can also depend upon the immediate reason for the analysis and the specific security being analyzed.

We have found that one-year time periods, updating range variabilities at least quarterly, are very useful for all time horizons. With many stocks, the high or the low, or both, projected on the basis of annual data available at the start of the period will be realized within the span of the first quarter of the projected year. The change in the price level results not only from co-movement of the stock's price with the market, but also adjustment of the price in response to available information, such as earnings forecasts. (The adjustment is not "instantaneous," as the modcaps believe.) By the end of the quarter new data will usually be available to indicate whether or not revised highs and/or lows are needed.

Current price, of course, is changing constantly, and risk and opportunity values along with it, so the effect of the CPF must be monitored often in order to assure the best timing of investment decisions. Even those investors with time horizons greater than one year (buy-and-hold types, for example) will find that monitoring on a short-term basis will be helpful in determining favorable buy-and-sell points. For the longer view, they can also calculate risk and opportunity for, say, a three- or five-year time span.

We are always glad to come across evidence to show that our approach, which can put shorter term investment on a logical basis, can also benefit those with a longer term investment philosophy. Probably the most successful of the buy-and-hold, growth-oriented mutual funds in the last decade or so has been New Horizons Fund of T. Rowe Price Associates, which performed so well that in 1972 it had to close its books to new investors. In 1973, however, up to May 10, it was down 28 percent, nearly four times as much as the market. The fund's president, Curran W. Harvey, told *Business Week* that one of the main reasons for the bad news was the failure "to cut back further on stocks which were either way overpriced and/or which had appreciated in amounts beyond our goal."[14] In our context, New Horizons continued to hold stocks even after they had reached levels of high risk and low opportunity. It can happen even to T. Rowe Price Associates.

Cyclical Stocks and Historical Averages

There is no single method which can be used with uniform success to determine future highs and lows of stocks. Nevertheless, there are basic approaches which when applied alone or, better, in combination to various classes of stocks can greatly improve the odds on successful prediction.

Cyclical stocks form one of these classes. American Telephone, the most widely held stock and the world's largest company, experienced three perfectly cyclical years at the end of a long, slow drop from the high levels of 1964. Knowing the highs and lows of 1970 (53⅞, 40⅜) and 1971 (53⅞, 40¾), a close approximation could have been made to the range of 1972 (53½, 41⅛), close enough to make quite accurate forecasts of risk and opportunity for that year. AT&T was also dependably cyclical, on a higher price level, for the years 1966 through 1969.

General Motors, to take another favorite of individual and institutional investors, has been cyclical since 1967. A good forecast of 1972 prices could have been made simply by averaging the highs and lows for the previous four years: a predicted high and low of 86 and 68, respectively, compared to the actual 84¾ and 71¼. These estimates are quite within workable (meaning useful) limits.

Many stocks are much more truly classifiable as cyclical than are AT&T and GM, which, based on earnings over the long term, are more like moderate growth stocks. For many stocks, where no reason for change is evident, and even when data are incomplete, it is possible to obtain workable figures for highs and lows simply by using the figures for the past year—or two or three. The key here is to select a past time span which is considered to be representative of the future period in question.

Morgan's Law and Its Corollaries

Our "Beta Mousetrap" article reported on part of a study we had made of a theoretical portfolio consisting of the 20 top favorites of institutional investors at that time, from IBM and Xerox down through Eastman Kodak and Avon Products. (The list has not changed much since that time.) The highs and the lows used for measuring the risk of the portfolio were the extremes (not annual averages) during a 3¼-year period, and we showed that even the stocks in this select group—which the pros certainly did not think of as cyclical—demonstrated a strong tendency to return toward the averages between their highs and lows. To quote from the article:

> The time period selected for determination of the highs and lows used in our calculations was 1968 through March, 1971, the point at which we measure the risk of the portfolio. This period encompassed a stirring sequence of boom, bust, partial recovery, depression and a second partial recovery. We have no evidence to prove that the next two or three years will not produce a similar variety of price movements, so until events indicate otherwise (and they haven't to date) we can assume that the time period selected is fairly representative of what lies ahead.
>
> Is it logical to assume that a stock will tend to return to its average price? Yes, because (among other things) of what we can call Morgan's Law: "The Market Will Fluctuate," and its corollary: "What Goes Up Must Come Down." Even IBM, the very epitome of the growth stock and still the fund managers' top choice, fell from around 358 on March 31 to a low of 283 in August, well below its 1968–71 average of 303. By year-end, 14 of the 20 stocks . . . had crossed their 3-year averages at least once, while four others came within a few points of doing so. The two big exceptions, explainable by persistent earnings trends, nevertheless experienced substantial moves toward their averages. Yet, sooner or later, they too must conform to Morgan's Law, just as the overall market must.

This tendency of stock prices to return to their averages might well be called *the French corollary,* after the oft-quoted Gallic observation, so far unchallenged even by modern capital market theorists, that "The more things change, the more they remain the same."

Projecting future highs and lows solely on the basis of past averages is the simplest method, and one subject to considerable error when unforeseen events occur. Nevertheless, over the long term it is bound to be right, for the simple reason cited, that what goes up must come down. The average high as well as the average low, just like the average of their mean, are measures of central tendency, which is to say that all will tend to return to their individual means. Here again, the importance of judgment in timing is evident.

Among the many stock data tabulated by the *Financial Weekly* are the highs and lows for the past 52-week and 5-year periods. These figures can be used to calculate risk and opportunity for those stocks whose future price ranges are deemed to be similar. (In fact, this method can give a useful and quick first approximation for almost any stock.)

In spite of the possibility of error in some cases, quantification of risk and opportunity using only the simple methods described above should increase the odds on successful results. These odds can be greatly improved by judgment as to when it is applicable and when to choose alternate approaches.

Trends in Prices

Another simple approach based solely upon historical prices can be applied to stocks in long-term uptrends. Modcaps to the contrary, the best stocks have enjoyed such trends for periods of several years, for the trends were based, not on the laws governing Brownian motion, but on sound evidence of growth and profitability. Going along with such trends has been profitable in the past and will be in the future. By projecting past highs and lows based upon persistent trends into the future, risk and opportunity can be measured, favorable buy-and-sell levels determined, and a vigil maintained to forewarn of the inevitable topping-out.

Although a corollary of Morgan's Law is "What Goes Up Must Come Down," its counterpart would need to be qualified as follows: "What Goes Down Must Come Back Up—Maybe." Some stocks, regrettably, like some of our best friends on the distaff side, have a limited period of appeal and popularity. Everyone is chasing them while they're hot, and then, in the title words of an old New Orleans jazz classic, it's "Go Back Where You Stayed Last Night, Baby, I Don't Want You No More."

Such stocks, along with others that may later enjoy a face lift, can show persistent downtrends, which may be tracked by risk and opportunity measurement. If the swings within downward sloping channels (to borrow the chartists' term) are wide enough, there may be some profit potential in the up phases, but these stocks are best left to the short sellers.

Trends in Price/Earnings Ratios

Up to now we have talked only about price trends. Other trends can also be helpful in setting highs and lows, notably trends of price/earnings ratios. Although some people would like to treat P/Es as immutable constants (ten-year averages, say, indicating where the price "should" be), they do have trends of their own, waxing with the increasing popularity of the stock and waning as enthusiasm cools.

IBM, although still selling at a hefty P/E ratio, is a good example of decline in recent years. The high/earnings and low/earnings ratios for the years 1968–72 were as follows:

	1968	*1969*	*1970*	*1971*	*1972*
H/E ratio.	49	45	43	40	39
L/E ratio.	36	36	25	31	30

Both the H/E and L/E ratios show steady erosion, the only anomaly occurring at the 1970 bear market bottom—a phenomenon shared by most stocks at the time. AT&T, however, stayed nearly on trend even through the 1969–70 bear market:

	1968	*1969*	*1970*	*1971*	*1972*
H/E ratio.	16	15	14	13	12
L/E ratio.	13	12	10	10	9

At the start of 1972, therefore, by using these trends plus available estimates of earnings, it was possible to arrive at quite accurate forecasts of highs and lows for the year. As always, judgment is necessary in projecting trends; they cannot continue forever, because they too have a central tendency over the long term. Both stocks mentioned, however, continued their downward trends into 1973.

The use of H/E and L/E trends to forecast highs and lows works best, as one would expect, on the more stable stocks. It does not work if there are sharp changes in earnings, earnings near zero, or net losses—when the P/E jumps to infinity.

Trends in Volatility

The two most important factors affecting the prices of most stocks, including their highs and lows, are (1) earnings and (2) overall market movements. Earnings—including not only absolute values, but rate of growth or decline and degree of variability—comprise the most fundamental factor in determining the price levels of a particular issue. Superimposed over the effect which earnings have on stock prices is the effect of general market movements, which can either accentuate or moderate the price ranges of individual stocks, that is, their highs and their lows. Range variability, or volatility, is a measure of all the factors that affect the price of a stock, including its earnings and general market movements.

The following Chapter 11 illustrates how co-movement with the market can be used to forecast prices. Chapter 12 shows how earnings are used to forecast highs and lows, which in turn are used to calculate risk and opportunity measures for investment decision making.

11

PREDICTING HIGHS AND LOWS: CO-MOVEMENT WITH THE MARKET

CO-MOVEMENT with the market is a simple and fairly effective approach to forecasting prices. The modern capital market theorists have conceived the beta coefficient as a measure of the degree of co-movement, and it can be used as such, although we don't agree that it's a good measure of risk. A beta of 1.0 indicates that the stock will move 10 percent for a 10 percent move in the general market. Betas of 1.5 and 0.5 mean movements of 15 percent and 5 percent, respectively, in response to a 10 percent market move. It follows that to use betas to forecast prices an estimate must be made of the amount which the market itself will advance or decline. (Those analysts who are keen on probability studies are free to make several estimates of market changes, weight each by its probability, and come up with an "expected value" to apply to the beta.)

Betas Can Help

We'll illustrate the method mainly with excerpts from a recent paper (unpublished) titled "Risk Measurement Reward: Betas Can Help Predict Short-Term Price Rises," in which we give examples of commercial betas along with our Poor Boy version, which is the ratio of a stock's range variability to that of the market.

The comparison of the commercial betas with the Poor Boy beta may not be quite fair, because the former are usually based upon rate of return rather than simple price change (Value Line is an exception), and they also use a variety of market indexes for their bases. Value Line's betas, for example, are keyed to its own index of the 1,400 stocks the survey covers. Standard & Poor's 500-stock index is often used as a base for commercial betas. The Poor Boy beta uses the NYSE composite average in this study.

Nevertheless, any broadly based index is in fact a well-diversified portfolio, so a True Believer in modern capital market theory might have reason to expect that the various bases for beta would produce about the same results. (Actually, the various betas show rather wide variations from source to source.) In addition, for the three-month period studied, dividends cause only minor differences between price volatility and rate of return variability.

A Study of the Dow Jones Industrials and Various Beta Sources

The study shows how advances in the prices of individual stocks conformed with their betas and the advance in the Dow during the first quarter of 1972. Specifically, it shows how the highs of the 30 components of the Dow Jones industrial average were related to the Dow's own high; how the rankings of price increases could have been forecast solely on the basis of beta rankings; how the best bets, or the highest risers, could have been predicted with a high degree of success; and how the selected beta sources performed.

Three well-known beta suppliers—Merrill Lynch, Value Line, and Jas. Oliphant—all performed quite well, as we shall see, in price prediction over the period examined. This, despite the fact that some research has indicated that beta, while dependably "stationary" (and therefore predictable) for large portfolios and longer time periods, is not predictable for individual stocks and short time periods.

Thus it may be that the real utility of beta, like beauty, is in the eye of the beholder, or as another bard put it, "In the rough marble beauty lies unseen," and but needs "the master's touch, the sculptor's chisel keen." While professing neither master's touch nor chisel keen, we are suggesting that a well-chosen variability measure might be even more useful than the warmest proponents of beta have claimed to date.

The values for all betas depend, of course, on the assumptions made in their calculation. Different assumptions as to time periods, market indexes, and so on can result in divergent values, as Table 11–1 demonstrates. General Motors, for example, is assigned a beta of 1.08 by Merrill Lynch, .71 by Value Line, and .90 by Oliphant. Although these three use similar methods of calculation, they agree on hardly any single stock. Even their averages, in fact, are widely divergent. Poor Boy betas are consistently higher than the others. The *relative* rankings show wide variations also, as we'll see in Table 11–3 on page 99.

TABLE 11–1
Beta Factors of the 30 Dow Jones Industrials

	Poor Boy	*Merrill Lynch*	*Value Line*	*Jas. Oliphant*
Allied Chemical	2.21	1.26	1.07	1.04
Alcoa	3.66	1.14	.96	1.19
American Brands	1.69	.77	.54	.53
American Can	2.47	.81	.74	.78
American Tel.	1.58	.81	.52	.65
Anaconda	3.98	1.04	.85	.96
Bethlehem Steel	2.30	1.02	.87	.78
Chrysler	1.76	1.52	1.38	1.74
Du Pont	1.13	.73	.61	.76
Eastman Kodak	1.86	.84	.75	.84
General Electric	2.03	1.17	.71	1.05
General Foods	2.05	.86	.71	.66
General Motors	1.23	1.08	.71	.90
Goodyear	1.44	1.00	.82	.67
Intl. Harvester	2.18	.85	.86	.86
Intl. Nickel	3.49	.88	.72	.67
Intl. Paper	2.00	1.21	.92	1.01
Johns-Manville	1.33	1.08	.89	.96
Owens Illinois	2.70	1.16	.74	1.20
Procter & Gamble	2.11	.83	.64	.46
Sears Roebuck	1.87	1.03	.76	.89
Standard Oil Cal.	1.42	.88	.67	.91
Standard Oil N.J.	1.18	.70	.54	.58
Swift	2.51	1.00	.84	1.15
Texaco	1.64	.91	.75	.90
Union Carbide	1.51	1.05	.91	.94
United Aircraft	3.39	1.25	1.08	1.46
U.S. Steel	2.04	1.00	.75	.80
Westinghouse	2.25	1.02	.90	.91
Woolworth	2.55	1.22	1.04	1.31
Average	2.12	1.00	.81	.92

Although betas based upon the last five years, the usual time period, may hold steadier over the years, for the purpose of forecasting over shorter time periods (3 to 12 months, say) the most practical assumption would seem to be that price volatility in the immediate past will continue into the immediate future. Therefore, the Poor Boy betas used in this example are based upon highs and lows for 1971 only, and they are tested, along with betas from the other sources, to determine if they could have been used to predict the price behavior of the 30 Dow stocks during the first quarter of 1972.

During that quarter the Dow index rose to a high of 950.18, a strong increase of 6.7 percent over the 890.20 at the end of 1971. If betas were a true measure of market sensitivity or co-movement during that time of generally rising prices, the percentage for each stock at its high should approximate the stock's beta multiplied by 6.7.

Results and Analysis

Table 11–2 shows the actual and projected highs for the 30 Dow Jones Industrials. In spite of the many differences in the betas from the various sources, the projected highs are generally quite close to those actually achieved. (All dollar and percentage figures in the tables have been rounded for easier comparison; the calculations were more precise.)

On average, the projected highs missed the actual highs by 3.1 to 3.6 points. A considerable part of the total error could be attributed to underestimating the rise of only two stocks, Du Pont and Kodak. In the light of *net* differences, Poor Boy's forecasts were closest to the actual rises—an overestimate of 0.5 point compared to underestimates of 2.7 to 3.3 points for the other beta sources.

Five Poor Boy projections were bull's-eyes, and only three were more than 10 percent wide of the mark: General Foods (13 percent high), Woolworth (12 percent high), and Du Pont (11 percent low). The other sources came closer on General Foods and Woolworth but were farther away on Du Pont.

The projections based on Merrill Lynch's betas included five bull's-eyes and six off the mark by 13 percent to 15 percent. Value Line scored three bull's-eyes and had six projections wide of the mark by 11 percent to 20 percent. Oliphant hit the most bull's-eyes (six) and

TABLE 11–2
Actual and Projected Highs during First Quarter 1972

			Projected High Based on Beta			
	Price 12/31/71	*Quarter High*	*Poor Boy*	*Merrill Lynch*	*Value Line*	*Jas. Oliphant*
Allied Chemical	29	32	33	32	31	31
Alcoa	44	54	54	47	46	47
American Brands	42	45	47	44	43	43
American Can	33	37	34	32	35	35
American Tel.	45	48	50	47	46	47
Anaconda	16	20	20	17	16	16
Bethlehem Steel	29	34	33	31	31	31
Chrysler	29	35	32	32	31	32
Du Pont	145	176	156	152	151	152
Eastman Kodak	97	120	109	103	102	103
General Electric	63	65	71	67	66	67
General Foods	36	36	41	38	38	37
General Motors	81	85	88	86	84	85
Goodyear	32	33	35	34	33	33
Intl. Harvester	30	32	34	32	32	32
Intl. Nickel	32	36	40	34	34	34
Intl. Paper	35	38	40	38	37	37
Johns-Manville	41	42	44	44	43	43
Owens Illinois	47	51	55	50	49	50
Procter & Gamble	79	90	90	83	82	81
Sears Roebuck	103	116	115	110	108	109
Standard Oil Cal.	57	61	63	61	60	61
Standard Oil N.J.	74	78	80	77	76	77
Swift	36	39	42	38	38	39
Texaco	34	36	38	36	36	36
Union Carbide	42	47	47	45	45	45
United Aircraft	29	37	36	32	32	32
U.S. Steel	30	34	34	32	32	32
Westinghouse	46	48	53	49	49	49
Woolworth	45	47	53	49	48	49
Average Difference from Actual High			3.1	3.4	3.6	3.3
Average Net Difference from Actual High			+0.5	−2.7	−3.3	−2.9

was 13 percent to 20 percent wide on six projections. Two of the wide misses by all three sources were Poor Boy bull's-eyes.

Forecasting Rankings

All of the projections of Table 11–2 were based upon the 6.7 percent rise in the Dow, which of course could not have been forecast precisely in advance. If the Dow had risen more or less than 6.7 percent, or had actually dropped, all prices would have been quite different—but the *order* of change should have remained the same, the stocks with the highest betas showing the biggest gains in up markets and the biggest drops in down markets. As a matter of practical investment strategy, then, it is only necessary to predict the direction of the market, not the amount of change. If the assumption had been made at the end of 1971 that the market was going to continue climbing, the best buys could have been forecast simply by ranking the stocks according to their betas, the stocks with the highest betas having the highest probability of exceeding the rise in the Dow.

Table 11–3 takes the betas of Table 11–1 and ranks them from 1 to 30. Anaconda, the top performer (up 31 percent), was ranked no. 1 by Poor Boy and 10 to 12 by the others. United Aircraft, no. 2, was ranked 4 by Poor Boy, 3 by Merrill Lynch, and 2 by both Value Line and Oliphant. No. 3, Eastman Kodak, missed by all, was ranked from 16 to 24. No. 4, Alcoa, was ranked 2 by Poor Boy, 8 by Merrill Lynch, and 5 by the others. And Chrysler, ranked 20 by Poor Boy and 1 by all others, came in a strong 5. Further comparisons, all down the line, are left to the reader.

If investment strategy had been to pick, say, the top five stocks, Poor Boy would have gained an average 20 percent; Merrill Lynch, 14 percent; Value Line, 18 percent; and Oliphant, 17 percent—all compared to a 25 percent gain of the actual top stocks and an average rise of 11 percent for the 30. Narrowing the choice to four stocks, Poor Boy would have scored 23 percent out of a possible 26 percent, and the others all 16 percent.

For those who wonder how this strategy might have worked over a longer time period (even without updating betas from quarter to quarter) we can report that relative rankings did not change very much for the full year 1972. Anaconda moved from 1 to 4, United Aircraft from 2 to 1, Kodak from 3 to 2, Alcoa from 4 to 8, and Chrysler from 5 to 3. Procter & Gamble moved up to 5 from 8 to join the top five. In what was an unusually big change in rank, International Harvester, rated 12 by Poor Boy, moved from 22 to 7.

In practice, all betas should be updated at least quarterly as the newest data are added and the oldest dropped. Betas based on five years' data will of course change slowly over time, while those based on only one year will be quicker to reflect the latest changes. In fact,

TABLE 11–3
Actual Price Increases and Projected Rank Based on Betas

			Beta Forecasts			
	Percent Increase at High	*Actual Rank*	*Poor Boy*	*Merrill Lynch*	*Value Line*	*Jas. Oliphant*
Allied Chemical	11	11	11	2	3	8
Alcoa	23	4	2	8	5	5
American Brands	8	17	21	28	28–29	29
American Can	10	14	8	26–27	19–20	21–22
American Tel.	7	19	23	26–27	30	27
Anaconda	31	1	1	12	12	10–11
Bethlehem Steel	17	7	9	14–15	10	21–22
Chrysler	22	5	20	1	1	1
Du Pont	21	6	30	29	27	23
Eastman Kodak	24	3	19	24	16–18	19
General Electric	4	28	16	6	22–24	7
General Foods	1	30	14	22	22–24	26
General Motors	5	23	28	9–10	22–24	15–16
Goodyear	5	26	25	16–18	14	25
Intl. Harvester	5	22	12	23	11	18
Intl. Nickel	11	13	3	20–21	21	24
Intl. Paper	7	18	17	5	6	9
Johns-Manville	2	29	27	9–10	9	10–11
Owens Illinois	10	15	5	7	19–20	4
Procter & Gamble	15	8	13	25	26	30
Sears Roebuck	14	9	18	13	15	17
Standard Oil Cal.	6	20	26	20–21	25	13–14
Standard Oil N.J.	6	21	29	30	28–29	28
Swift	8	16	7	16–18	13	6
Texaco	5	27	22	19	16–18	15–16
Union Carbide	11	12	24	11	7	12
United Aircraft	27	2	4	3	2	2
U.S. Steel	13	10	15	16–18	16–18	20
Westinghouse	5	24	10	14–15	8	13–14
Woolworth	5	25	6	4	4	3

the responsiveness to current conditions of the Poor Boy beta used is what gave it its edge in making short-term forecasts. (We have already indicated that in using betas for short-term forecasting we are enlarging on what has been considered their normal use, measuring portfolio risk, and in this sense may be rating them unfairly.)

Summary and Conclusions

In summary, all of the beta sources reviewed proved to be reasonably good guides for projecting both price highs in absolute figures and relative price increases in the short-term market tested here. It is not surprising that a few stocks did not fit the general pattern. It is rather surprising—because of the many other factors working to affect prices—that so many stocks did conform to the simple rule that those with the highest volatility are, measurably and ratably, the best bets in a rising market. Much more statistical work would have to be done, of course, to support the general conclusion (although it may sound like an article of faith to some modcaps who do not draw fine distinctions between short and long term, individual stock and portfolio betas, price volatility and rate of return).

The above study demonstrated how co-movement with the market could be used to forecast highs, one of the variables in risk and opportunity measurement. Future lows can be estimated in the same way, by estimating the low for the market index used and multiplying the beta of each stock by the percentage drop in the market.

As we have stressed, this is a simplistic technique, and it should be used along with the various alternate approaches described in this book in order to give proper weight to other important price determinants. Current price, for example, can be incorporated by calculating how much a stock is under- or overpriced and applying the correction to the change due to co-movement.

12

PREDICTING HIGHS AND LOWS: ESTIMATED EARNINGS

As INDICATED in Chapter 10, since both earnings and earnings trends are among the most influential determinants of stock prices, estimated earnings, along with trends in the ratios of high/earnings and low/earnings, can be used to forecast highs and lows.

High and Low Price/Earnings Ratios

If we make the assumption that historical H/E and L/E ratios are a reliable guide to the next period, we can—given earnings estimates—forecast high and low prices. Let's say we're at the end of 1971, and we have Value Line's earnings estimates for Du Pont for 1971 (not yet reported by the company) and for 1972 (understandably subject to even more error). The figures are $7.10 and $7.90, respectively. If we believe that the general market in 1972 will have no more effect upon Du Pont's price range than it had in 1971, we can assume the same range variability and therefore the same H/E and L/E ratios.

The projected high (to the nearest dime) would be: 7.90/7.10 times the 1971 high, 158.0 = 175.8, and the projected low 7.90/7.10 times the 1971 low, 129.5 = 144.1. During the first quarter of 1972 Du Pont, which ended 1971 at 145, hit an actual high of 175.5 and a low of 144.3.

This example represents an extraordinarily good adjustment of prices to anticipated earnings—even though the latter turned out to be somewhat wide of the mark. Note that the adjustment was not "instantaneous," as it would be in the "efficient market" of the modern capital market theorists. There was plenty of time to assess risk and opportunity and to profit from the market move.

When the returns were finally in, Du Pont's earnings were actually 7.33 for 1971 and 8.50 for 1972. Had the final figures been available earlier, the yearly high of 184.4 could have been approximated as follows: $8.50/7.33 \times 158.0 = 183.2$.

We have called this an extraordinary example, and it is exactly that. Prediction usually is not so simple, for many other factors can affect stock prices. Nevertheless, the method indicates how the important factor of earnings can be utilized in forecasting prices.

Applying the Method to the Dow 30

To continue with the illustration and application of this method, let's assume that we are a new and hungry management and research organization looking for some pension fund money with which to establish our reputation. We present our case to several chief financial officers (CFOs) who are responsible for allocating the pension fund assets of their corporations. Usually we are told that the trustee of the pension fund is the same bank that makes loans to the company when it needs money, and they naturally want to maintain a warm relationship, because who knows when they'll need another loan? But one of the CFOs finally admits some dissatisfaction with his bank-trustee, which has managed to underperform the market for most of the past decade, even though its expertise has been given a free hand.

Okay, says the hard-nosed CFO; we'll give you a piece of this money to run on a trial basis, but with certain constraints: (1) Your "approved" or "restricted list" is the 30 Dow Jones Industrials; (2) Your method must be simple and clearly stated at the start; (3) All money must be fully invested on the last trading day of 1971, and there will be no trading or second-guessing during the first quarter of 1972. At the end of the quarter we'll check your record and see where we go from there.

Severe constraints indeed, but we accept them (we're hungry, remember?). We've already explained to the CFO our method of measuring risks and opportunity, so we tell him, All right, here's our method. We'll rate the 30 stocks for opportunity and buy the top 20 percent (six stocks is about the minimum for effective diversification), allocating an equal amount of money to each stock. We'll assume the same range variabilities for 1972 that existed in 1971 and project highs and lows on the basis of estimated earnings for both years, as published by Value Line in late 1971.

One necessary qualification: If the projected 1972 low is much above the price at 1971 year-end, we know it can't adjust that much overnight, and it may even go down a bit, so for our projected low we'll use the year-end price less 10 percent and adjust the projected high to maintain constant range variability. (Rationale: other factors are at work temporarily more powerful than forecast earnings, but the pull of higher earnings will be felt sooner or later.)

Performance

At the end of the quarter, we report that our portfolio, consisting of the six stocks rated tops for opportunity, is up 12.6 percent, compared to an average rise of 4.3 percent for the 30 stocks on our restricted list, and only 2.2 percent for the remaining 24 stocks. The DJI index (which has become oddly weighted over the years) is up 5.7 percent and the NYSE composite index, up 5.8 percent.

The portfolio, therefore, has performed 5.7 times as well as the average of the 24 stocks rejected for having too little opportunity; 2.9 times as well as the average stock in the Dow 30; and 2.2 times as well as the market, as measured by the DJI and the NYSE composite indexes.

Outperforming the NYSE average by 120 percent is commendable in the light of the small size of the restricted list and the fact that the really big winners on the Big Board were not among the Dow 30.

Our simple method of selection (ratings for all stocks will be given after this summary) spotted three of the stocks which came out on top in actual performance at the end of the quarter, as the following tables show.

Performance of Actual Portfolio

Stock	*Predicted Rank*	*Actual Rank*	*Percent Gain*
Anaconda	1	2	20.0
Alcoa	2	6	14.2
Intl. Nickel	3	13	5.3
United Aircraft	4	8	11.6
Owens Illinois	5	11	7.5
Bethlehem Steel	6	4	17.2
Average Gain			12.6

Performance of Ideal Portfolio

Stock	*Actual Rank*	*Percent Gain*
Eastman Kodak	1	20.9
Anaconda	2	20.0
Chrysler	3	18.2
Bethlehem Steel	4	17.2
Du Pont	5	17.2
Alcoa	6	14.2
Average Gain		18.0

Analysis of Results

Although the method correctly rated Anaconda, Alcoa, and Bethlehem Steel among the top six performers, it missed Kodak, Chrysler, and Du Pont. However, it substituted three stocks which performed well above average, so that the portfolio return, 12.6 percent, amounted to 70 percent of the 18.0 percent obtainable with perfect predictive powers.

There is no doubt that much better performance could have been obtained without the constraints, which were much more onerous than any imposed on portfolio managers (with the possible exception of stock/bond ratios). For example, a wider field for screening and selection would have resulted in top stocks with much higher opportunity, as we'll demonstrate later when we consider a few of the institutional darlings. Also, the use of additional criteria for forecasting highs and lows, and for selection, would have helped.

Another severe constraint was in the rigid timing of purchases and sales. In actual practice, even if the approved list were restricted to the 30 stocks of the Dow, tracking of risk and opportunity values would have revealed better buy-and-sell points, as we can see in Figures 12–1, 12–2, and 12–3 (see pages 110–12). Alcoa, for example, which dropped down almost exactly to its predicted low, could have been bought at lower risk and higher opportunity. High-volatility Alcoa, Anaconda, and United Aircraft might well have been sold at greater profit before their price retreats if the upper limit of risk had been set at, say, 0.5.

Du Pont, one of the top performers missed by our simple screen, might well have been purchased if risk and **O/R** ratio had been among the criteria for selection. Kodak could have been included when its price dropped. Considerations of quality and the desire to minimize overall risk of the portfolio could also have favored the selection of Du Pont and Kodak. Both of these stocks, along with Chrysler, the third big miss, later reported much better 1972 earnings than the estimates on which the price forecasts were made. Chrysler, for example, reported $4.25, 31 percent higher than the estimate we used.

This brief postmortem was not offered solely as an alibi for the misses; it was also meant as a review of some of the important practical considerations which arise in active portfolio management, as well as an indication of the dynamism implied in the use of risk and opportunity techniques. (We'll have more to say about the quantitative method in the next chapter, when we detail the important steps in portfolio management.)

The complete story on each of the 30 stocks is detailed in Tables 12–1 and 12–2. The reader can spend as much or as little time on these as he wishes. Figures 12–1, 12–2, and 12–3 present a visual summary of the 30, each **O/R** diagram showing 10 stocks.

Considering the "brute force" nature of our approach, there seems to be remarkable conformity between projected and actual (1) highs and lows, (2) rankings for appreciation at subsequent highs, and (3) rankings for depreciation at subsequent lows. In an up market, projections for highs can be expected to show closer correlation than projections for lows. Also, the correlations between predicted rankings and actual rankings should be closer for the first quarter than for the year, because expectations change as new earnings estimates and other pertinent data come in. Many of the misses can be explained on the basis

TABLE 12–1
Predicted and Actual Prices

Company	Symbol	*1972, 1971 Earnings* Estimated	Actual	*1971* High Low End	*1972* Est. High Low	Average	RV	CPF	*1st Quarter* High Low End	Percent Change	*1972* High Low End	Percent Change
		2.25	2.38	34.6	38.9				32.4	+11.3	36.8	+26.5
Allied Chemical	ACD	2.00	1.88	23.4	26.3	32.6	.387	–.215	27.8	– 4.5	26.1	–10.3
				29.1					30.9	+ 6.2	29.0	– 0.3
		4.20	4.61	70.0	76.1				53.6	+22.9	57.3	+31.4
Alcoa	AA	2.50	2.45	36.0	39.2	57.7	.640	–.489	38.9	–10.8	38.9	–10.8
				43.6					49.8	+14.2	53.1	+21.8
		4.60	4.52	49.8	52.1				45.1	+ 7.6	49.3	+17.7
American Brands	AMB	4.40	4.30	37.0	38.7	45.5	.295	–.158	41.9	0.0	39.6	– 5.5
				41.9					43.8	+ 4.5	42.1	+ 0.5
		2.90	2.95	45.9	46.6				36.8	+10.2	36.8	+10.2
American Can	AC	2.50	2.66	29.6	30.1	38.4	.430	+.260	32.0	– 4.2	27.0	–19.2
				33.4					33.4	0.0	31.6	– 5.4
		4.20	4.34	53.9	55.9				47.9	+ 6.9	53.5	+19.4
American Tel.	T	4.05	3.92	40.8	42.3	49.1	.277	–.175	42.6	– 4.9	41.1	– 8.3
				44.8					43.3	– 3.3	52.8	+17.9
		1.00	2.00	27.8	28.9				20.3	+31.0	21.9	+41.3
Anaconda	A	0.05	0.28	11.5	14.0	21.5	.693	–.558	15.6	+ 0.6	15.6	+ 0.6
				15.5					18.6	+20.0	19.5	+25.8
		3.50	3.02	30.5	42.7				34.0	+17.2	34.6	+19.3
Bethlehem Steel	BS	2.50	3.14	20.3	28.4	35.6	.402	–.371	28.3	– 2.4	25.1	–13.4
				29.0					34.0	+17.2	29.4	+ 1.4
		3.25	4.27	33.4	35.0				35.0	+22.4	41.6	+45.5
Chrysler	C	1.85	1.67	24.5	25.7	30.4	.306	–.118	28.0	– 2.1	28.0	– 2.1
				28.6					33.8	+18.2	41.0	+43.4
		7.90	8.50	158.0	175.8				175.5	+21.0	184.4	+27.2
Du Pont	DD	7.10	7.33	129.5	144.1	160.0	.198	–.188	144.3	– 0.5	144.3	– 0.5
				145.0					169.9	+17.2	177.5	+22.4
		3.05	3.39	100.0	115.1				120.3	+23.6	149.8	+54.0
Eastman Kodak	EK	2.65	2.60	72.0	82.9	99.0	.325	–.034	93.3	– 4.1	93.3	– 4.1
				97.3					117.6	+20.9	148.4	+52.5
		2.70	2.91	66.5	69.1				65.0	+ 3.8	73.0	+16.6
General Electric	GE	2.60	2.60	46.5	48.3	58.7	.354	+.133	58.3	– 6.9	58.3	– 6.9
				62.6					64.6	+ 3.2	72.9	–16.5
		2.60	2.20	44.3	48.0				36.1	+ 0.6	36.3	+ 1.1
General Foods	GF	2.40	2.26	30.8	33.4	40.7	.359	–.236	28.3	–21.2	23.5	–34.5
				35.9					28.5	–20.6	28.5	–20.6
		7.05	7.51	91.1	97.3				84.8	+ 5.3	84.8	+ 5.3
General Motors	GM	6.60	6.72	73.4	78.4	87.9	.215	–.168	76.8	– 4.6	71.3	–11.4
				80.5					84.3	+ 4.7	81.1	+ 0.7
		2.65	2.65	35.3	39.0				33.1	+ 4.7	33.5	+ 6.0
Goodyear	GT	2.40	2.34	27.4	30.3	34.7	.251	–.179	29.5	– 6.6	26.5	–16.1
				31.6					31.3	– 0.9	31.5	– 0.3
		2.00	3.17	33.9	39.6				31.5	+ 5.4	40.5	+35.5
Intl. Harvester	HR	1.40	1.65	23.0	26.9	33.3	.381	–.204	26.8	–10.4	26.8	–10.4
				29.9					27.1	– 9.4	38.4	+28.4
		1.90	1.47	46.8	54.3				35.5	+10.6	36.6	+14.0
Intl. Nickel	N	1.45	1.26	24.9	28.9	41.6	.610	–.457	29.8	– 7.2	29.4	– 8.4
				32.1					33.8	+ 5.3	31.9	– 0.6
		2.10	2.30	40.6	48.7				37.5	+ 7.1	42.3	+17.3
Intl. Paper	IP	1.75	1.53	28.5	34.2	41.5	.349	–.313	33.6	– 4.0	33.3	– 4.9
				35.0					36.6	+ 4.6	41.9	+19.7
		2.75	2.66	46.1	46.3				41.6	+ 2.0	41.6	+ 2.0
Johns-Manville	JM	2.40	2.49	36.5	36.7	41.5	.232	–.034	35.0	–14.2	27.4	–32.8
				40.8					38.8	– 4.9	31.3	–23.3

TABLE 12–2
Predicted and Actual Ranks

	Gains						Losses					
			Actual Ranks						Actual Ranks			
			1st Quarter		All Year				1st Quarter		All Year	
Company Symbol	*Opportunity*	*Predicted Rank*	*At High*	*At End*	*At High*	*At End*	*Risk*	*Predicted Rank*	*At Low*	*At End*	*At Low*	*At End*
ACD	.602	10	11	12	10	23	.172	12	18	19	14	8
AA	1.129	2	4	6	8	9	.151	17	6	25	12	22
AMB	.453	17	17	17	16	21	.137	18	28	14	21	10
AC	.690	7	14	20	24	25	.170	13	19	11	4	6
T	.452	18	19	23	14	13	.102	22	16	8	17	18
A	1.251	1	1	2	4	7	.135	19	30	29	30	24
BS	.773	6	7	4	15	18	.031	28	24	27	8	13
C	.424	20	5	3	3	3	.188	9	25	28	27	28
DD	.386	21	6	5	9	8	.010	29	27	26	29	22
EK	.359	24	3	1	2	1	.291	6	20	30	24	30
GE	.221	30	28	19	20	14	.487	2	11	12	19	17
GF	.595	11	30	30	30	28	.123	20	1	1	1	3
GM	.383	22	23	15	27	19	.047	25	17	16	11	12
GT	.430	19	26	21	26	22	.072	24	12	10	6	9
HR	.585	12	22	28	7	6	.177	10	7	3	13	25
N	1.067	3	13	13	23	24	.153	16	11	18	16	7
IP	.662	8	18	16	18	10	.036	27	21	15	23	21
JM	.266	28	29	25	29	29	.198	8	2	6	3	2

TABLE 12–1
Predicted and Actual Prices (continued)

		1972, 1971 Earnings							*1st Quarter*		*1972*	
Company	*Symbol*	*Estimated*	*Actual*	*1971 High Low End*	*1972 Est. High Low*	*Average*	*RV*	*CPF*	*High Low End*	*Percent Change*	*High Low End*	*Percent Change*
		4.10	3.95	66.3	71.5				50.9	+ 9.5	54.6	+17.4
Owens Illinois	OI	3.80	3.62	41.0	44.2	57.9	.472	–.394	43.0	– 7.5	40.5	–12.9
				46.5					50.0	+ 7.5	41.8	–10.1
		3.30	3.38	81.3	92.2				90.0	+14.6	112.8	+43.7
Procter & Gamble	PG	2.91	2.91	56.0	63.5	77.9	.368	+.015	76.1	– 3.1	76.1	– 3.1
				78.5					88.6	+12.9	111.5	+42.0
		3.85	3.93	104.1	116.2				116.3	+13.5	119.6	+16.7
Sears Roebuck	S	3.45	3.56	74.8	83.5	99.9	.327	+.052	97.4	– 5.0	97.4	– 5.0
				102.5					113.5	+10.7	116.0	+13.0
		6.20	6.45	63.4	67.2				60.8	+ 6.1	82.1	+43.3
Standard Oil Cal.	SD	5.85	6.02	49.5	52.5	59.9	.245	–.087	54.0	– 5.8	54.0	– 5.8
				57.3					55.5	– 3.1	79.6	+38.9
		7.15	6.83	82.4	88.6				77.9	+ 5.6	89.3	+21.0
Standard Oil N.J.	J	6.65	6.77	67.0	72.0	80.3	.207	–.162	68.0	– 7.9	68.0	– 7.9
				73.8					70.3	– 4.7	87.5	+18.6
		2.90	2.90	45.0	49.1				38.8	+ 7.8	39.5	+ 9.7
Swift	SWX	2.66	2.00	28.8	31.4	40.3	.439	–.213	32.0	–11.1	30.3	–15.8
				36.0					33.0	– 8.3	39.4	+ 9.4
		3.65	3.27	39.6	43.1				36.0	+ 4.7	39.1	+13.7
Texaco	TX	3.35	3.32	29.6	32.3	37.7	.286	–.175	30.0	–12.8	29.5	–14.2
					34.4				30.9	–10.2	37.5	+ 9.0
		2.80	3.42	50.4	55.3				47.0	+11.1	52.0	+22.9
Union Carbide	UK	2.55	2.53	38.6	42.4	48.8	.264	–.264	41.9	– 0.9	41.9	– 0.9
					42.3				44.5	+ 5.2	50.0	+18.2
		3.75	4.17	45.1	48.3				37.3	+26.9	49.0	+66.7
United Aircraft	UA	3.50	3.62	24.5	26.2	37.3	.592	–.424	28.6	– 2.7	28.6	– 2.7
					29.4				32.8	+11.6	44.5	+51.4
		3.85	2.90	35.9	39.2				34.1	+12.5	34.8	+14.9
U.S. Steel	X	2.35	2.85	25.0	27.3	33.3	.357	–.180	30.4	+ 0.3	27.4	– 9.6
					30.3				33.5	+10.6	30.5	+ 0.7
		2.10	2.24	48.9	51.3				48.3	+ 5.2	54.9	+19.6
Westinghouse	WX	2.00	2.08	32.8	34.4	42.9	.394	+.140	43.0	– 6.3	38.4	–16.3
					45.9				47.8	+ 4.1	43.0	– 6.3
		2.80	2.60	55.3	59.0				47.3	+ 4.9	47.3	+ 4.9
Woolworth	Z	2.65	2.50	35.5	37.5	48.3	.445	–.133	39.6	–12.2	30.3	–32.8
					45.1				42.5	– 5.8	31.3	–30.6

of earnings forecasts. (For comparison, the final figures—not available, of course, at the time the forecasts were made—are listed in Table 12–1 adjacent to the estimated earnings.)

R/O Diagram Analysis

The three **R/O** diagrams, Figures 12–1, 12–2, and 12–3, give a vivid picture of what happened to each of the Dow Jones 30 during the first quarter. The heavy lines indicate the range of risk and opportunity values for each stock between high and low prices during the

BLE 12–2
dicted and Actual Ranks (continued)

	Gains						Losses					
			Actual Ranks						Actual Ranks			
			1st Quarter		All Year				1st Quarter		All Year	
pany nbol	*Oppor- tunity*	*Pre- dicted Rank*	*At High*	*At End*	*At High*	*At End*	*Risk*	*Pre- dicted Rank*	*At Low*	*At End*	*At Low*	*At End*
....	.866	5	15	11	17	27	.078	23	9	20	10	4
....	.353	25	8	7	5	4	.383	3	22	24	25	27
....	.275	27	9	9	19	15	.379	4	15	22	22	16
....	.332	26	20	22	6	5	.158	15	19	9	20	26
....	.369	23	21	24	12	11	.045	26	8	7	18	20
X..........	.652	9	16	27	25	16	.226	7	5	4	7	15
....	.461	16	27	29	23	17	.111	21	3	2	9	14
....	.528	15	12	14	11	12	.000	30	26	17	28	19
....	1.016	4	2	8	1	2	.168	14	23	23	26	29
....	.537	14	10	10	21	20	.177	11	29	21	15	11
....	.254	29	24	18	13	26	.534	1	13	13	5	5
....	.578	13	25	26	28	30	.312	5	4	5	2	1

quarter. If forecasts for the year had been completely fulfilled during the quarter, the heavy line would completely cover the lighter volatility line. As the key of Figure 12–1 shows, starting positions are indicated by a heavy dot, and positions at the end of the quarter by a transverse line. The NYSE composite index is included for comparison.

Most of the stocks stayed within their predicted ranges, that is, above the zero risk line and to the right of zero opportunity. Two major exceptions were General Foods, which dropped $5 lower than predicted, and Kodak, which outdid itself on the upside by the same amount. When limits are exceeded, of course, it means that the projec-

FIGURE 12–1
Risk/Opportunity Diagram (Allied Chemical through Eastman Kodak)

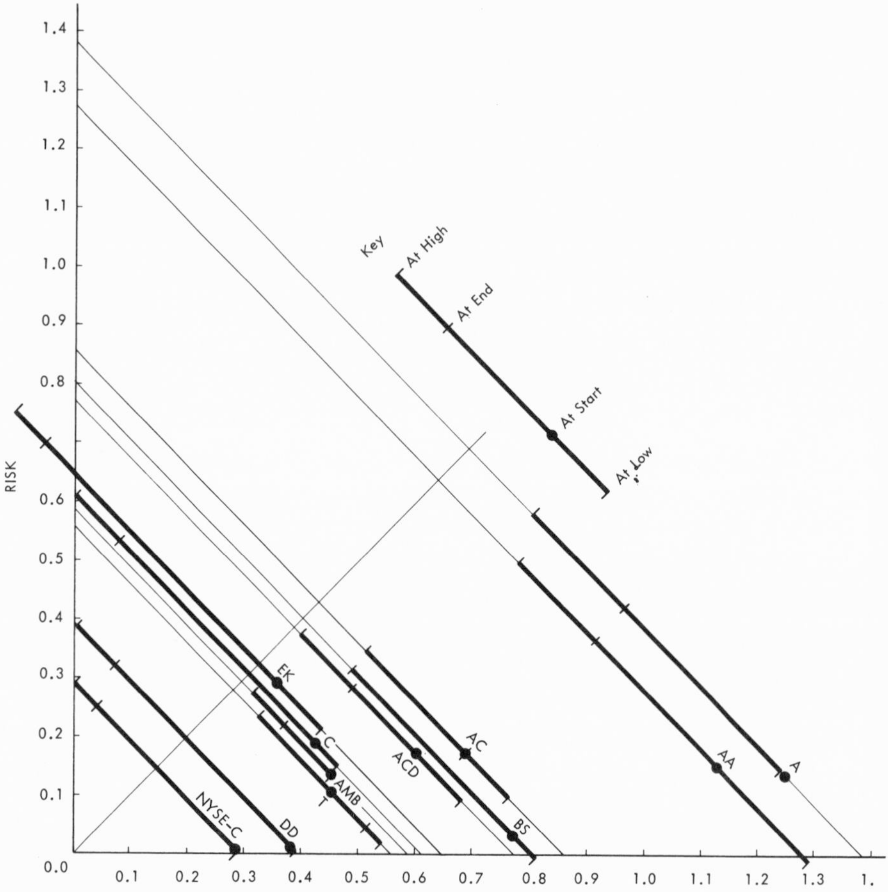

See Tables 12–1 and 12–2 for meanings of symbols

tions were in error for one reason or another, so new calculations are in order.

Most stocks dropped down close to, or below, their predicted lows. Seven, including Kodak, got up near their predicted highs during the quarter (and seven more before the year was out).

With the help of the **R/O** diagrams and study of the starting positions (denoted by the dots), there is no difficulty in spotting potential winners, such as Anaconda and Alcoa, in the high-opportunity area; and pullbacks GE and Westinghouse in the low-opportunity area.

IGURE 12–2
isk/Opportunity Diagram (General Electric through Procter & Gamble)

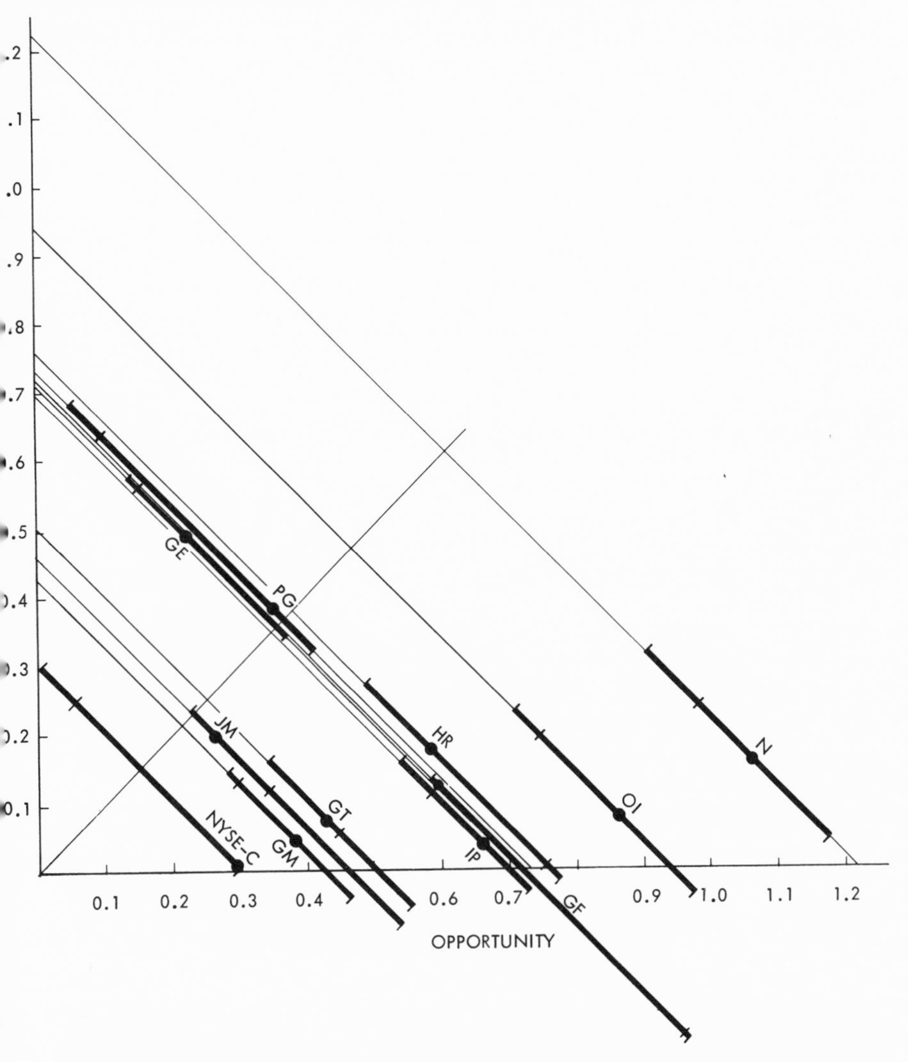

A detailed analysis of the tables and diagrams developed in our study of the 30 stocks, and the relationship of each detail to stock selection, timing, and so forth, could become very involved indeed and still seem simple when compared to the real world of stocks. Fortunately, the application of the method is much simpler than its detailed explanation. Once all relevant data have been distilled into risk and opportunity measures for a selected period, the rest—using the basic

FIGURE 12–3
Risk/Opportunity Diagram (Sears Roebuck through Woolworth)

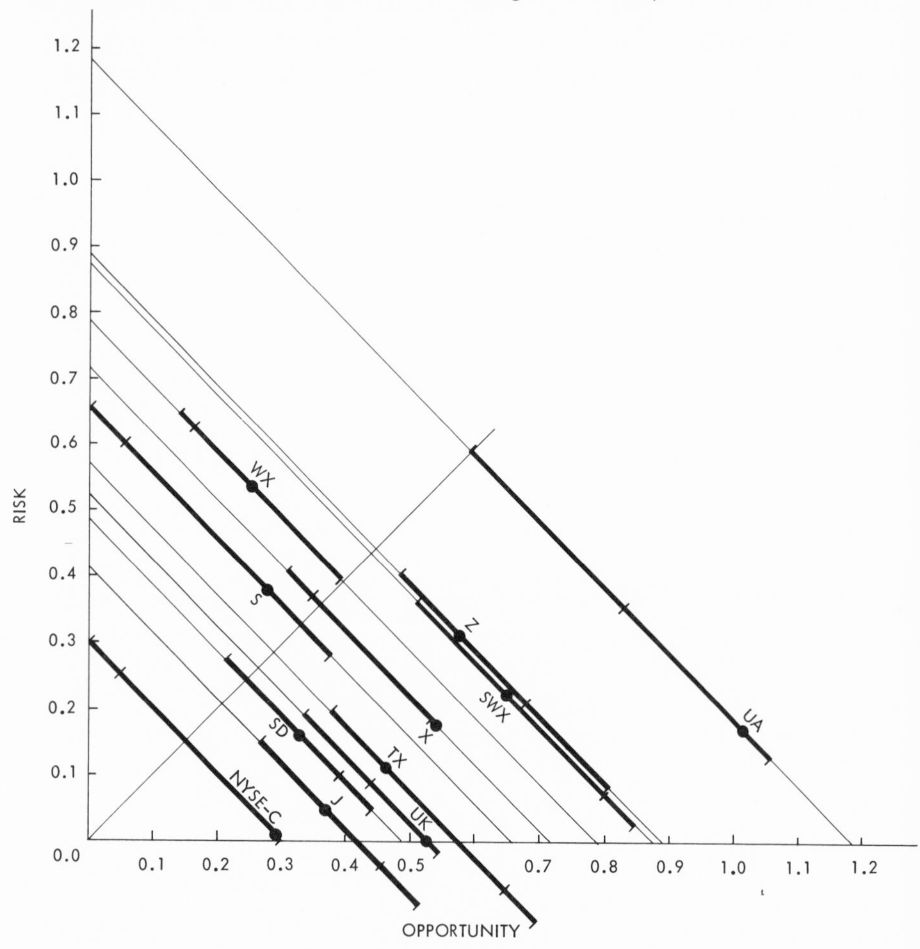

principles described in this book—is quite straightforward. The procedure is set forth in Chapter 13, to which we turn after a brief look at a few darlings of the institutional investors.

Testing a Few of the Institutional Favorites

The 30 Dow Jones Industrials—the restricted list we have just examined—were for the most part a sedate lot, advancing only 4.3 percent on average. Let's look now at the same method of forecasting highs and lows for a racier group, a few of the institutional favorites.

We'll take six stocks—IBM, Polaroid, Avon Products, Reynolds Industries, Burroughs, and Warner-Lambert—and compare them with four stocks on the Dow list that are also held in huge amounts in institutional portfolios—General Electric, Sears, Du Pont, and Westinghouse.

Forecasting Prices

As before, 1972 highs and lows have been forecast by multiplying 1971 highs and lows by the ratio of estimated earnings for the two years.

Table 12–3 shows the ten stocks, listed in approximate order of popularity among institutional investors, along with (1) estimated earnings—upon which the forecasts were based, (2) actual earnings—for comparison, (3) actual 1971 prices, (4) estimated highs and lows for 1972, (5) range variabilities and current price factors as of the end of 1971, and (6) actual prices for 1972, with percentage price changes for the first quarter.

The first quarter, as we know, is the period during which much of the expected price change may be realized; after that, fresh forecasts, based upon new inputs, are often necessary. (*First quarter* in the general sense means that of the year forecast, not necessarily the calendar year.) It is left to the reader to examine the table in order to check actual prices against those forecast. Many are remarkably close.

As in our earlier example, it seems that stocks are trying their best to conform to the modcaps' idea of an efficient market, but as usual, it takes a while, and there's plenty of time to take advantage of under- or overpricing.

Table 12–4 shows the risk, opportunity, and **O/R** ratios for the ten stocks, and the resultant rankings for projected price increase and decrease at quarterly high, low, and end.

Ranking Highs

The projections for rankings of subsequent highs based on opportunity rankings were almost perfect, especially for the leaders and lag-

TABLE 12–3
Predicted and Actual Prices

		1972/1971 Earnings						*Actual Prices*		
								1st Quarter		
Company	*Symbol*	*Estimated*	*Actual*	*1971 High Low End*	*1972 Est. High Low*	*RV*	*CPF*	*High Low End*	*Percent Change*	*197 High Low End*
		10.25	11.03	365.8	407.5			386.0	+14.7	426
Intl. Bus. Mach. .	IBM	9.20	9.38	283.3	315.6	.254	–.139	331.8	– 1.4	331
				336.5				382.3	+13.6	402
		2.70	2.90	66.5	69.1			65.0	+ 3.8	73
General Electric .	GE	2.60	2.60	46.5	48.3	.354	+.133	58.3	– 6.9	58
				62.6				64.6	+ 3.2	72
		3.85	3.95	104.1	116.2			116.3	+13.5	119
Sears Roebuck. .	S	3.45	3.54	74.8	83.5	.327	+.052	97.4	– 5.0	97
				102.5				113.5	+10.7	116
		2.00	1.30	117.1	126.6			127.1	+42.8	149
Polaroid	PRD	1.85	1.86	76.0	82.2	.425	–.295	86.1	– 3.3	86
				89.0				124.0	+39.2	126
		7.90	8.50	158.0	175.8			175.5	+21.0	184
Du Pont	DD	7.10	7.33	129.5	144.1	.198	–.188	144.3	– 0.5	144
				145.0				169.9	+17.2	177
		2.10	2.30	48.9	51.3			48.3	+ 5.2	54
Westinghouse . .	WX	2.00	2.08	32.8	34.4	.394	+.140	43.0	– 6.3	38
				45.9				47.8	+ 4.1	43
		2.20	2.16	112.0	133.2			119.3	+18.8	139
Avon Products. .	AVP	1.85	1.89	82.1	97.6	.308	–.260	94.0	– 6.4	94
				100.4				115.0	+14.5	136
		5.70	5.32	69.5	77.7			75.0	+29.3	78
Reynolds Ind. . .	RJR	5.10	5.10	50.3	56.2	.322	–.269	58.3	+ 0.5	47
				58.0				72.1	+24.3	51
		4.45	4.71	159.9	175.7			173.0	+13.2	229
Burroughs	BGH	4.05	4.03	104.5	114.8	.419	+.103	146.0	– 4.5	146
				152.8				163.9	+ 7.3	217
		3.10	3.16	82.0	90.8			87.1	+ 9.1	100
Warner-Lambert.	WLA	2.80	2.81	67.1	74.3	.199	–.068	77.1	– 3.4	77
				79.8				83.8	+ 5.0	97

gards: five bull's-eyes and four misses by a margin of one. Only Du Pont missed by two, coming in third compared to a fifth place forecast. Actual rankings for the end of the quarter were the same as those for the high.

Rankings by **O/R** ratio were also quite predictive, especially for the laggards. Du Pont, ranked too low by opportunity, was ranked too high by **O/R**.

ABLE 12–4
edicted and Actual Ranks

				Gains–Ranks				*Losses–Ranks*			
				Predicted by		*Actual at*		*Predicted by*		*Actual at*	
ompany Symbol	*Oppor-tunity*	*Risk*	*O/R*	*O*	*O/R*	*High*	*End*	*R*	*R/O*	*Low*	*End*
IBM	.393	.115	3.42	4	5	5	5	7	6	8	6
GE	.221	.487	0.45	10	10	10	10	3	1	1	1
S	.275	.379	0.73	7	7	6	6	4	4	4	5
PRD	.720	.130	5.54	1	4	1	1	6	7	7	10
DD	.386	.010	38.60	5	1	3	3	10	10	9	8
WX.	.254	.534	0.48	9	9	9	9	1	2	3	2
AVP	.568	.048	11.83	3	2	4	4	9	9	2	7
RJR	.591	.053	11.15	2	3	2	2	8	8	10	9
BGH	.316	.522	0.61	6	8	7	7	2	3	5	4
WLA	.267	.131	2.04	8	6	8	8	5	5	6	3

Ranking Lows

The rankings for subsequent lows based upon risk were also quite close, especially considering that the maximum down movement, that of GE, was only 6.9 percent. Avon, ranked ninth, but coming in second, was the only major deviation, and by the end of the quarter, it had moved back to seventh. **R/O** ratings, in general, were close to target for both quarterly lows and ends.

Selecting the Winners

The various criteria for portfolio selection will be considered in the following chapter, but in this case simply picking the two stocks rated highest for opportunity, Polaroid and Reynolds, would have been quite rewarding. They finished first and second, with an average gain of 36 percent at their highs and a 32 percent gain at the end of the quarter.

R/O Diagram

Figure 12–4 depicts the history of each stock during the quarter. Du Pont is not shown because its volatility line almost coincides with

FIGURE 12–4
Risk/Opportunity Diagram—Some Institutional Favorites

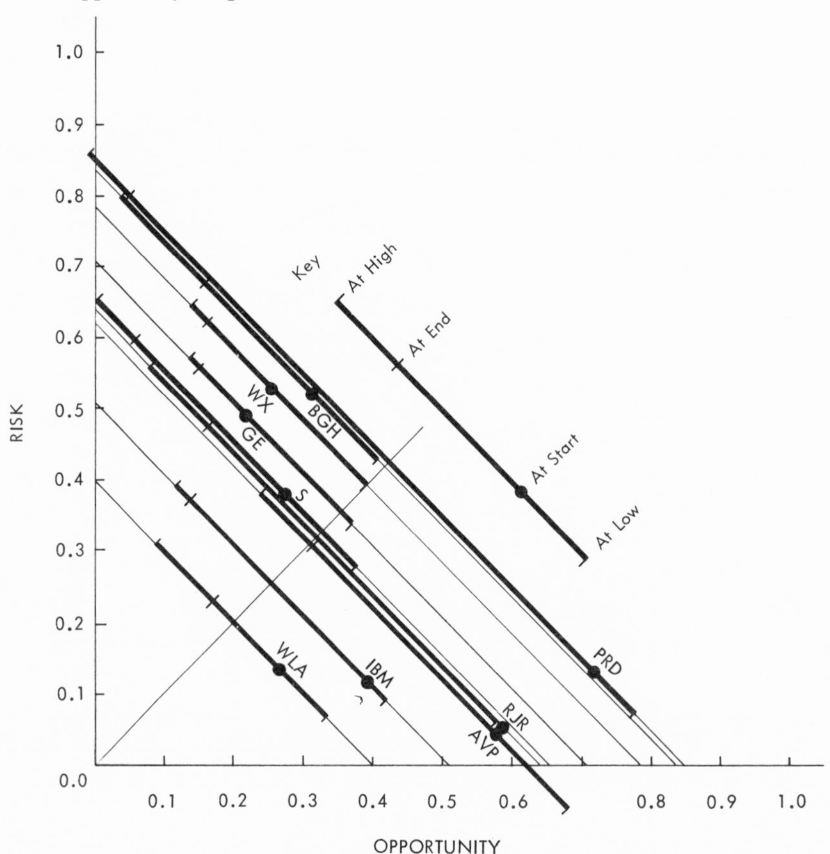

that of Warner-Lambert (Du Pont appears in Figure 12–1). Again, Polaroid and Reynolds are obviously the best selections for potential gains, because at the start they lie in the high-opportunity/low-risk area, and both fulfilled their expectations by quickly climbing into the low-opportunity/high-risk area. Avon, ranked third, came in fourth. Its reported 1972 earnings dropped a bit under those projected; that's really bad news for a growth stock selling at Avon's astronomical P/E. Interestingly, the earnings of both Polaroid and Reynolds failed to meet expectations by substantial margins and were good sells at their low-opportunity highs for the quarter; both suffered big pullbacks in subsequent quarters. The bad news was out in plenty of time to adjust risk and opportunity values and take profits or sell short. Even without any news or recalculation, both stocks were treading on thin ice before the end of the first quarter.

Conclusion

Although we have applied the method to other stocks and time periods in our private work, critics will say, not without some justification, that the above examples are selected ones, and do not constitute statistical proof over a long time period. We suggest, therefore, that interested statistical analysts put this approach to the test. In fact, we're more than willing to do the job ourselves if we can get financial backing and computer access through the largess of some foundation, university, pension fund, bank, broker, investment management group, oil sheik, or Goldfinger. (At the present time, all we have is a desk calculator and a thousand ideas for research.)

We must emphasize again that no simple, brute force method will hold up very long, especially after a lot of people get into the act.

Nonetheless, for all its simplicity, the method just demonstrated may be better than any simple approach yet devised, and when used along with the other tools suggested in this book, it has a useful place in portfolio management. Earnings are, in fact, a solid base for the quantification process. Top results will be realized by those best able to (1) build on and modify this base through analysis of the other factors discussed herein and (2) apply the system of portfolio management we take up now.

13

A QUANTITATIVE METHOD OF PORTFOLIO MANAGEMENT

AN EFFICIENT PORTFOLIO, by our definition, is one with maximum opportunity for a given level of risk or one with minimum risk for a given level of opportunity.

Through the use of the risk and opportunity measures already described, it is possible to devise *and maintain* efficient portfolios to meet the objectives of every investor, from the most speculative-minded to the most risk-averse, from the short-term trader to the buy-and-hold pension fund, and from the bond or income fund to the high-performance growth fund.

Obviously, risk and opportunity are tradeoffs when a stock is selling near its average price, but the ratio of one to the other can vary over a wide range, depending upon current price. The quantification of risk and opportunity allows the portfolio manager to take maximum advantage of these inevitable swings.

We have already demonstrated, in the foregoing chapters, the individual techniques needed for a logical, quantified system for managing assets consisting of marketable securities. Although the emphasis was on common stocks, the method can be applied to any assets with variable, quoted values. Even assets with fixed value, such as cash, can of course form a part of the portfolio. Cash, having both risk and opportunity values equal to zero, lessens both overall risk and opportunity of a portfolio in proportion to the amount of cash relative to variable assets.

Portfolio management can be divided into six basic steps: (1) measurement, (2) comparison, screening, selection, (3) timing, (4) monitoring and control, (5) maximizing return with minimum risk, and (6) review and adjustment. All six steps are interrelated and constantly interacting.

Step One: Measurement

This is the basic step upon which the validity of the others rest. It is also by far the most difficult. Everything that might affect the future behavior of each individual stock must be distilled here into two numbers—the projected high and the low—which are in turn used to quantify risk and opportunity. It is not only fundamental data about a company which are assessed in this step, but also all information concerning related companies, industry and the economy, the effect of stock market movements upon the price of the stock, the time horizons for both projected prices and portfolio policy, and in the final analysis—because factual data are never complete—the need to apply to it all some degree of probabilistic, common-sense, or intuitive modification.

Most of this book is concerned with the techniques and application of measurement. Some useful approaches have been suggested for forecasting highs and lows, but it is up to the investor, whether individual or institutional, to complete the process. The importance of data gathering and storage, research, and competent and rapid assessment and quantification is obvious. Because risk and opportunity values change—rapidly with current price and more slowly with range variability—the measurement step must be almost continuous to be most effective.

Step Two: Comparison, Screening, Selection

This step takes the various risk and opportunity measures resulting from step one, compares them on the basis of absolute and relative values, screens out stocks with risk above and opportunity below selected limits, and ranks the rest in order of opportunity, risk, **O/R** ratio, risk/market, and so on. Other screening criteria set by management (e.g., quality, minimum company sales volume, debt structure, number of shares out, or whatever) are applied, and the result is the select list of stocks which meet all criteria. The top stocks in the select list are evident from their rankings.

Because stocks can move on or off the select list solely on the basis of current price, it will save time to apply the screening criteria to a larger "approved list" of stocks which meet other more or less stable criteria as to quality and so forth, instead of screening every stock in the universe.

Step Three: Timing

Portfolio performance and management efficiency rest importantly upon the timing of purchases and sales, whether stocks are held for years or only days. The quantification of risk and opportunity makes possible profitable trading on price swings of shorter duration than might otherwise be considered, and at the same ameliorates the trauma induced in traders by the dread affliction called "whipsawing." We are definitely not advocating go-go operations or short-term trading of the knee-jerk variety. We are advocating taking advantage of wide price swings by selling when **R/O** ratios are measurably excessive and buying when **O/R** ratios are high.

Despite the current popularity of bond and other income funds, few investors will disagree with the statement that the profit *potential* in stocks lies predominantly in the magnitude and frequency of price swings. The quantification of risk and opportunity brings closer the realization of that potential. Even if the realization is only partial, appreciable savings or gains can result if the risk and opportunity figures are anywhere close to reality.

For some investors, taxes must be considered in making timing decisions. This nuisance can be monitored in step four and acted upon in step five. Taxes are no problem for the largest pools of capital, the "qualified" pension funds; and management would have to be lax indeed to have failed to obtain government qualification for tax exemption, which hinges mainly on the access of all employees to the pension plan.

Step Four: Monitoring and Control

This step takes the outputs from steps two and three and tracks them (1) to make sure that the stocks in the portfolio stay within the prescribed limits, (2) to monitor the total risk and opportunity of the portfolio, weighting each asset with its current market value, (3) to compare stocks in the portfolio to others on the select list, (4) to devise and compare alternative portfolios, and (5) to track portfolio performance.

Monitoring and control overlap steps five and six, where further comments will be made.

Step Five: Maximizing Return with Minimum Risk

This is the action step in which the decisions are made on the basis of the other steps in order to maintain maximum portfolio efficiency under whatever criteria have been set. We have used the word *return* here instead of *opportunity,* because it is the reward that we are really seeking, the bottom line after risks are taken and opportunities are seized or missed. High returns are realized only by taking action—buying and selling—based upon risk and opportunity values (and these, as we have seen, can include dividends and other cash income).

Considerations of Portfolio Efficiency

The process of maintaining "maximum portfolio efficiency" must be tempered with reason and practicality. First of all, we must avoid what we call "Markowitz' dilemma," the conclusion that the most efficient portfolio consists of one stock—the one most highly rated by the criteria selected.

Diversification

A certain amount of diversification must be maintained in order to reduce the chance of getting clobbered by a single stock. We have said little about diversification in this book, because it is so easy to achieve, and because the subject has been adequately covered by other writers. For even large portfolios, nearly perfect diversification can be obtained as easily with 20 stocks as with 100 or 1,000. Common sense tells us that all 20 stocks should not be in the shoe industry nor in computer leasing.

Allocation of Assets

A decision related to diversification is determining just what proportion of total assets is to be allocated to each stock, or between stocks and bonds, if the latter form part of the portfolio. We believe that bonds, and all other investment alternatives, should be subjected to the same risk and opportunity analysis as that applied to stocks, using the same selection criteria (and of course taking cash income into account).

This might well rule out bonds for portfolios seeking better than average income. However, if one of the constraints on the portfolio manager is that he must allot a certain percentage of funds to bonds, he could make the best of the situation by maintaining *two* efficient portfolios, one for stocks and one for bonds, each with its own selection criteria. Overall risk and opportunity would be determined by giving appropriate weights to the assets in each portfolio.

Switching

Another pragmatic consideration in maintaining portfolio efficiency lies in the fact that changing prices will probably reveal theoretically more efficient portfolios almost every trading day—more often than it is practical to switch, for reasons such as transaction costs and taxes. No switch should be made on the basis of small differences in the risk and opportunity values. A general rule, in fact, is to stay with the good performers until there is clear reason to sell, even though, as the price of a stock moves up, risk increases and opportunity decreases. This fact points up the need for constant tracking. A stock can be held for long periods of time if it continues to perform well; continuous revision of the risk and opportunity measures in the light of unfolding information will keep it within acceptable limits during the entire period.

Flexibility

The efficient portfolio, then, will have some flexibility. Although its longer term aim remains "the biggest bang for the buck," it may not, at every moment in time, represent the most perfect theoretical efficiency possible.

The limits set for portfolio control may also vary somewhat along with external factors. For example, in bull markets more risk may be tolerated on the way up, and less opportunity accepted. In bear markets, less risk may be acceptable, and more opportunity required. However, little or no adjustment in the guidelines is necessary if the measures are kept truly up to date, for projected highs and lows will take into account co-movement with the market.

As bull markets peak and prices head downward, risk and opportunity will dictate switching from long to short positions, where opportunity is high and risk is low. Sad to say, however, the vast majority of organized funds, and some not so organized, cannot or will not engage in short selling, so they operate under a serious constraint, unable to take advantage of high opportunity. The usual method of cushioning the blow is to increase the cash position, both by doing some selling and by sitting on any new cash, such as regular additions to pension funds (that is, putting it into Treasury bills and other near-cash securities). The big institutional funds have the added constraint of illiquidity; if they tried to liquidate on a large scale the whole ball game would be over. Therefore, they have no choice except to ride out bear markets, agonizing helplessly as they watch the bulk of their vast holdings sink in value, trying to moderate the disaster by going into cash positions which seldom exceed 5 percent or 10 percent of their assets; switching, to whatever extent possible, into less volatile issues; and finding what consolation they can in the thought that the long-term trend of the market is up (or at least used to be).

Funds operating under such conditions obviously cannot take full advantage of the opportunities presented by the quantification methods described herein, but they *can* use them to maximize the utility of all actions possible within their constraints. That is, their buying and selling—while amounting to only a small fraction of total assets—is still huge in absolute amount, and both should be timed on the basis of measured risk and opportunity. In fact, it is especially important for the big funds, because of the restricted opportunity just described, to use all of the steps of portfolio management outlined in this chapter, adhering to them as closely as their particular constraints will allow.

Liquidity problems also mount with institutional concentration on a relatively few favorite stocks—a current situation loaded with risk.

Risk and opportunity considerations might help the institutional giants ease out of this trap over time by allocating more money to companies they are now neglecting. The medium- and small-sized firms, after all, need financial support more than the monsters. We must not lose sight of the main reason for the existence of the stock market, which is to supply capital where it is needed.

Control Models

The concept of portfolio management using quantification of risk and opportunity is represented by Figure 13–1, a version of the familiar risk/opportunity diagram, with guidelines for portfolio management superimposed. The guidelines depicted here are simple: (1) no stock is purchased with less than 0.20 opportunity or more than 0.15 risk and (2) every stock is sold before risk reaches 0.75 or opportunity drops to 0.20.

These limits define the buy-and-hold areas for every stock on the select list, whether or not in the portfolio at the present time. Low volatility stocks—those with range variabilities under 0.1—are excluded, but every stock with an RV over 0.1 and risk under 0.15 is a candidate for purchase if not already in the portfolio.

In appreciation potential, stocks become increasingly attractive as we move toward the right side of the buy area, because the **O/R** ratio increases in that direction; the potential also increases with nearness to the zero-risk line at the base. For practical reasons (because of the short distance between buy and sell points) stocks falling in the extreme left side of the buy area would not be attractive. Such stocks could be eliminated from consideration by a minimum appreciation guideline or higher RV cutoff.

The hold area delineates risk and opportunity values while stocks are held for appreciation (and—let's face it—during price pullbacks, unless a stop-loss rule is operating). Every stock is sold before risk reaches 0.75 or opportunity drops to 0.20. Sales or switches into better values can, of course, be made at any point in the hold area before the limits are reached.

Under the limits postulated, most stocks could be held even after rising above the **R** = **O** line, that is, even after they became "overpriced." Those with range variabilities between 0.4 and 0.6 could be held into the higher **R/O** areas. Those with low RV's would be sold because of their relatively low appreciation potential after they rise

FIGURE 13–1
Control Model for Portfolio Management

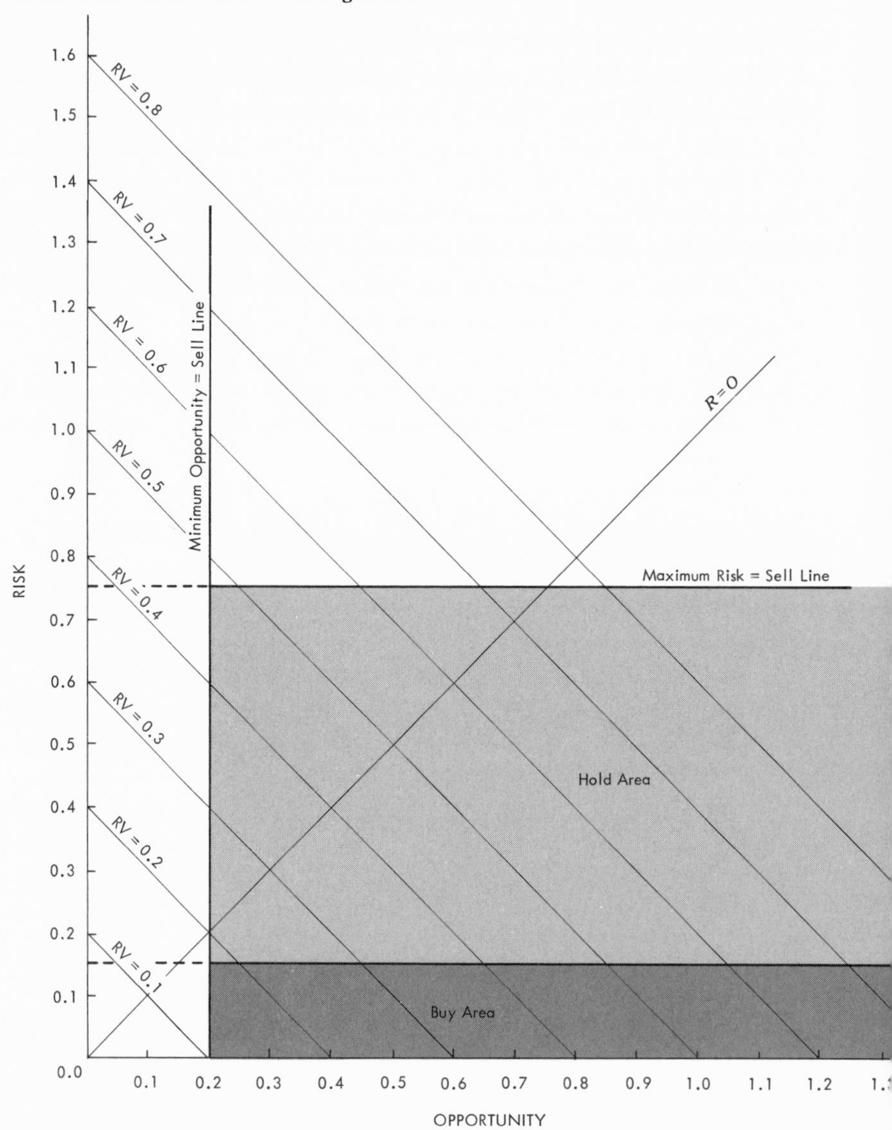

much above the **R** = **O** line; those with high RV's would be sold to avoid the danger of big pullbacks. The volatile stocks with RV's greater than 0.7 would be eliminated shortly after going through their projected average prices; those with RV's of 0.8 would be eliminated even before this happened.

In effect, the guidelines say: It's okay to invest in highly volatile stocks provided you buy in at the right price and get out while the getting's good. In short, don't be greedy with the highfliers.

As indicated, guidelines are set in accordance with overall portfolio policy regarding risk limitation and performance goals, but they still have some flexibility. Let's assume that you are a portfolio manager for a pension fund and you receive another one of the periodic cash infusions from your client. The market has been moving up for some time, and most of your stocks—thank God—are nicely up in the hold area. In fact, there are no good stocks in the buy area; otherwise you'd already have done some switching. Under these circumstances the alternatives are to sit on the cash (in CDs or Treasury bills) until the market drops way down again or put the money into stocks which still have good appreciation potential. If the fundamentals (earnings, money supply, GNP and so on) indicate a continuation of the bull market, the risk guideline can be relaxed, and the money invested in the lowest risk stocks falling in the hold area—very likely the same ones already in your portfolio if you've been maintaining an efficient one.

Many other modifications are possible in setting risk and opportunity limits for portfolio management. Figure 13–2 illustrates how risk/opportunity ratios can be used to modify the simple pattern of Figure 13–1. Now the buy area is decreased by the guideline that no stock will be purchased unless its **O/R** ratio is 5/2 or more, but still no stock is bought if its risk exceeds 0.15. This puts a positive limit on risk for the most volatile stocks, while assuring greater appreciation potential for those with lower volatility. The sell lines are modified by the rule that no stock is held beyond an **R/O** ratio of 3/1, which limits the risk of holding high-rising stocks of the middle volatility range too long.

Another possible modification (not illustrated) would be a limit placed upon volatility, say a maximum RV of 0.6, which would eliminate from consideration all stocks falling to the upper right of the RV = 0.6 line in Figure 13–2.

R/O diagrams, with whatever guidelines may be set, have their equivalents in computer printouts. The latter are a necessity when the select list is large.

Another helpful variation in applying the risk/opportunity concept is the use of risk/market and opportunity/market ratios instead of the simpler measures just illustrated. Stocks, when plotted, still have

FIGURE 13–2
Modified Control Model for Portfolio Management

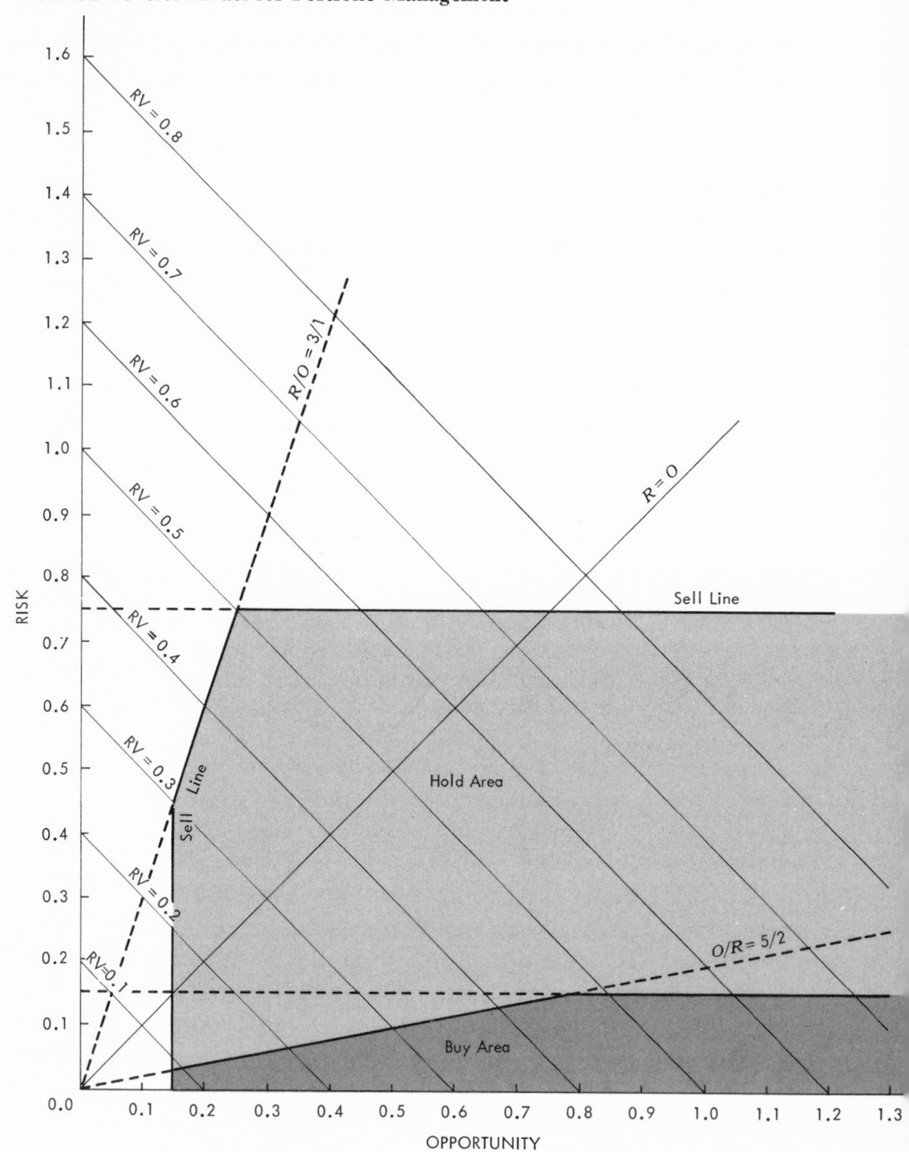

the same relative positions on the diagram, but the different guidelines, now set relative to the current market, add another dimension.

R/O and market-related diagrams can be used to track entire portfolios (of mutual funds, say) as well as individual stocks. Guidelines will not be the same for portfolios as for stocks. Because diversification moderates both risk and opportunity, tighter guidelines are in order to delineate the smaller acceptable portfolio area (corresponding to the hold area for stocks). The risk limit, for example, would be higher for acceptable stocks than for the portfolio as a whole, because high-risk stocks can be balanced by those with low risk to reduce the overall risk of the portfolio.

There are two methods, both helpful, for using our measures to calculate portfolio risk and opportunity. One is to weight the figures for each security by its current asset value and then to determine the weighted average. This average, based upon projected highs and lows, is useful in looking to the future as well as for current monitoring and control. The other way, useful in comparing present risk and opportunity with the historical record, and also testing the accuracy of forecasts made in the past, is based upon actual highs and lows realized during selected time periods.

In summary, step five—the action step—integrates the output of all the other steps in the portfolio management process, including the following and final one.

Step Six: Review and Adjustment

The review is backward looking, assessing portfolio performance and the effectiveness of guidelines, techniques, sources of information, brokers, analysts, and portfolio managers. In the light of the review, forward-looking decisions are made on any adjustments which may be needed in risk and opportunity guidelines, general techniques, brokers, analysts, and portfolio managers.

14

SHORT SELLING AND HEDGING

No discussion of portfolio management would be complete without some description of the technique of selling short and of the hedge funds which use the technique as an integral part of their operations.

The Long and the Short of It

Because stock prices, perversely, go down as well as up, and because short selling is the only way to make money in a bear market, we believe that the failure to use short selling in the portfolio management program is akin to entering a foot race and using only one foot. Hedging against market reversals by investing a part of portfolio assets in short positions is really the most logical and the only comprehensive method of portfolio management, and the one offering consistently the greatest opportunity for profit along with the least risk.

We have shown that, as stock prices rise, risk increases and opportunity decreases for the long type of investment we have been discussing throughout most of this book. Just the opposite is true for short positions. Near bull market tops, therefore, most longs are much riskier than shorts. In order to maintain a truly efficient portfolio it is necessary to shift from long positions to short ones as the bull market booms along and opportunity shifts from the longs to the shorts. Just the opposite course is necessary in bear markets.

The risk and opportunity measures we have developed, along with some other hedge fund management techniques we shall explain in the next chapter, make it possible to determine at any moment what proportion of total assets should be in longs and what proportion in shorts. In fact, the risk and opportunity measures presented in this book evolved out of our study of hedge funds, *Hedgemanship: How to Make Money in Bear Markets, Bull Markets and Chicken Markets While Confounding Professional Money Managers and Attracting a Better Class of Women.*[64]

A *chicken market,* in case you haven't heard, is one whose future course in unknown, i.e., the market which exists on every trading day. All those who embrace the random-walk theory should be grateful for the term, but so far they've failed to show their appreciation.

There are ways, as *Hedgemanship*'s subtitle suggests, to stay in tune with, and profit from, any kind of market, and we'll discuss them in the next chapter.

First, however, because there is such enormous prejudice against short selling, let's explore that subject. In November 1970, not long after the 1969–70 bear market and the concurrent wave of brokerage house failures had shaken the investment world, *Barron's* published our "Primer for Shorts: How to Survive and Even Prosper in a Bear Market."[65] In the light of the current bear market (as we write this in mid-1973), the article seems almost prescient, so we'll repeat and adapt some of it now as a means of reviewing some basic facts about short selling.

The Fundamentals of Short Selling

The recent stock market disaster [the article begins] has given convincing proof once again that virtually no investor, amateur or professional, knows how to profit—or even avoid losses—in a bear market. Let's ask the reader who, like the vast majority, lost money during the long market decline: Don't you wish you had held short positions in the very stocks in which you were caught long? You'd have *gained* about the same amount you lost, and as a result you'd no doubt be a lot easier to get along with—cherished by family, friends, associates, and merchants.

It's too late, regrettably, to do much about your recent losses—but will you be ready for the *next* bear market? You will concede, surely, that another bear market *is* coming, and still others after that, just as certainly as night follows day—although perhaps without the same nicety of timing.

Contrary to just about universal belief, selling short—at least so far as the investor himself is concerned—need to be no more complicated than buying long. Furthermore, short selling need involve no more risk than buying long. All those who wish to avoid trauma in future bear markets, and even prosper in them, might now—before being swept up by a new wave of optimism—set aside the usual bias long enough to consider again the subject of short selling.

The Simple Side of Selling Short

A short sale is made in the expectation that the price of the stock will decline. For example, 100 shares of Pat-A-Kake Franchise Systems is sold short at 50. If the stock declines to 40 and is bought or "covered" at that price, the profit is $1,000 (less the usual brokerage fees and transfer tax). If the price goes up to 60 and the short sale is covered there, a loss of $1,000 results.

The short seller must, sooner or later, complete the transaction by buying the same number of shares he sold short.

Short sales can be made only on the "uptick" or the "zero-plus" tick. In other words, the price at which the short sale is made must be at least one eighth of a point higher (the uptick) than the preceding transaction in that stock, or at the same price as the preceding transaction (zero-plus tick) if *that* was higher than the preceding different price. This rule was designed to moderate the depressing effect that short selling might otherwise have on a declining stock.

The Dark Side of the Market

Short selling has been called "the dark side of the market," and even worse. Many people seem to feel instinctively that short selling is the embodiment of evil. Even our government discriminates against it. The SEC, with its uptick rule, tries to restrain short selling; even if a profit is made, it is subjected to harsher tax treatment than long-term gains made by buying long.

No objections are raised if a profit is made by buying a stock and selling it later. This is considered normal, constructive, and fully in accord with the Protestant, Judeo-Christian, and any other known ethic. However, if these two simple actions—buying and selling—are done in reverse order, which is all that short selling amounts to, attitudes undergo a profound change. This is sinister, destructive, unethical, and—apparently—un-American, in the view of at least two official agencies of the U.S. government.

Most of the objection to short selling appears to be a holdover from the era of the Robber Barons, based on subliminal memories of the ruthless bear raids of such bad guys as Jim Fisk, Jay Gould, and Dan Drew. But in a later and even more disastrous era, that of the Great Crash, Joseph P. Kennedy added to his already large assets by selling short. This was before the uptick rule was conceived to moderate bear markets, when short selling could accelerate price drops. However, apparently not enough stigma was attached to Mr. Kennedy's bear market activities to prevent his appointment as first head of the SEC, an agency formed by the then-new Roosevelt administration to crack down on the bad guys of Wall Street; nor has public indignation been evidenced by refusal to elect three of Mr. Kennedy's sons to high office.

The Brighter Side

It would be appropriate to exorcise at least some of the devils who seem to have taken over the nether world of short selling. We might even discover that some of the spirits-in-residence are benevolent.

Putting prejudice aside for a moment, let's consider some fundamentals. Markets go up; markets go down. You needn't go back as far as 1929 to know that markets go down. You know markets go down if you reached an age of awareness before 1962, or even 1966—and that should include almost all of you, with the possible exception of a few of the youngest portfolio managers. For them, we had 1969–70.

Not only do markets go down, but also the prices of individual stocks go down, often even in upside markets. Every market day, no matter what the overall trend, records its declines as well as its advances, its downside as well as its upside volume, and usually new lows as well as new highs.

That being so, everyone should have the inalienable, unfettered right to believe that a stock will, on occasion, go down—and the right to risk his own money to back that opinion. There should be no more restriction on selling short than on buying long. Both involve a purchase and a sale; only the timing is different. To handicap short selling is much like saying that it's all right to bet your money for the football team you think is going to win, but you mustn't bet against a team you think will lose.

The uptick rule, by hampering short selling, does perhaps serve a useful purpose by moderating downside markets. But a "downtick" rule—which not even the SEC has proposed—would make much more sense during runaway upside moves, which have caught a lot more people and cost them a great deal more money than can ever be blamed on short selling.

Is it immoral or sinister to sell a stock with the expectation that its price will go down to some point where one can buy it and show a profit? Hardly. The short seller believes that the price of a particular stock will decline, and he may even be hoping and praying that it will do so, but he is not praying for the collapse of the whole economy. Generally speaking, his morality could probably be compared favorably with that of an administration which uses government powers to tighten the financial screws on everybody in order to "cool the economy." Besides, the typical investor has his longs as well as his shorts to worry about; he's not praying for universal disaster.

Before we leave the subject of public morality and the common weal, let's ask: Why shouldn't a part of the citizenry (the short sellers) be happy and making money even during bear markets? Must we all be depressed at the same time?

Even the most practical of economic considerations would seem to demand a substantial short position in the stock market. Think how all the curves of the economic indicators would be smoothed out if half, say, of all investors were making profits during bear markets.

A high short position, furthermore, represents future demand, and therefore gives strong support to the market itself. There is an additional important function that active short selling performs: it lends liquidity to the market by helping to satisfy demand, which is, after all, what a free market is all about. A short seller, be it remembered, is not forcing his stock on the buyer. The buyer believes that the stock is going up—and he might well be right.

Bias against Short Selling

These are some of the reasons why short selling *should* be given the same consideration and treatment as buying long. In practice, of course, it is not. The uptick rule is applied to short selling; there is no downtick rule for buying long. All capital gains made by selling short, even if the position is held more than six months, are taxed as regular income; profits on long positions held over six months are taxed as long-term gains.

There is not much the investor can do about the uptick rule, although it does not apply to unlisted stocks, and the Pacific Exchange, for one, does not enforce it for odd-lot, i.e., up to 99-share, short sales of listed stocks. The investor can attempt to overcome the effect of higher taxes on short selling by more frequent turnover, since there is no inducement to hold on for long-term gains. This tactic is favored by the fact that declines often take place over a shorter timespan than the equivalent upswings. Long-term tax treatment for a short position *can* be obtained by purchasing a put option, holding it over six months and selling it before the exercise date.

The general prejudice against short selling could be based in part on the risk involved. Central to the risk story used to frighten would-be short sellers is that possible losses on short positions are unlimited. On a long position, the maximum loss is 100 percent, even if the price goes to zero; but with a short the theoretical loss could be 1,000 percent if the stock goes from 10, say, to 110. In practice, however, the short seller can control his loss by covering at any point in the rise where he chooses to get out and limit his loss.

The Mechanics

The mechanics of short selling are simple enough as far as the investor is concerned, even for the uninitiated. If the stock is trading at about the level at which he wishes to take a short position, the seller simply tells his broker: Short 100 Tulipmanix Corp., or whatever, at the market. The broker does the necessary paper work, and the stock is sold on the next uptick or zero-plus tick.

It is of little concern to the short seller, but the broker, in order to make delivery to the buyer, must borrow the 100 shares somewhere, either within his firm or from an outside lender. The money value of the stock is sent by the broker to the lender and held as collateral until the short sale is covered and the stock is replaced.

Short sales are subject to the same margin requirements as long purchases. No margin is required if the short seller also holds securities convertible into the stock.

No interest is charged on short positions taken on margin, because the proceeds from the sale are enough to supply the collateral required by the lender of the stock. (In fact, when the borrowed stock comes from another account with the same firm, the broker enjoys interest-free use of the proceeds, which he can lend back to his own margin customers at 9 percent or 10 percent interest.)

If dividends or any other benefits are payable on the stock during the time the short position is held, the short seller must reimburse the lender of the stock. This should be no deterrent to the short seller; a stock selling exdividend is, at least theoretically, worth less than before the amount of the dividend, and this fact is frequently reflected by an adjustment in the market place.

When little demand exists for the loaned stock, the lender may pay interest on the collateral he holds. Ordinarily, however, no interest is paid, and when there is great demand for the stock, the lender may even demand a premium. Stocks for which a premium is required should be avoided by the short seller; if the supply is that tight, it indicates the danger of a "squeeze" at the time of covering.

Every month, usually five business days following the 15th, the total short interest of every listed stock having a short position of 20,000 shares or more is reported, along with those showing a change in short position from the previous month of at least 10,000 shares. These figures, along with the previous month's, are published in *Barron's, The Wall Street Journal,* and other periodicals. The number of listed shares for each NYSE stock also is given.

As the short position gets greater in relation to the number of shares outstanding, the risk of a short-covering squeeze increases. The trend of the short interest can be estimated by comparing month-to-month figures. Those stocks "possibly involved in arbitrage" are also noted, and this fact of course reduces somewhat the importance of the short total, because the arbitragers will not add materially to a short-covering squeeze.

Highfliers and Gliders

"Highfliers" are those stocks with high volatility, high turnover, high price-earnings ratios, and, quite often, high short interest positions relative to the number of shares outstanding. They are very tempting stocks to sell short and they are very dangerous. A simple, dogmatic rule: Lay off the volatile highfliers while they're flying, even if you *know* they're overvalued on a fundamental basis.

Other caveats: Avoid any stocks with a high short interest; otherwise you may be shot down in the cross fire between the computerized gunslingers. Avoid companies with a small number of shares, especially if they are closely held; covering the short could be costly. Avoid stocks with very low trading volume; a fairly active market is desirable for short covering. Avoid, if you can, potential takeover candidates, which are likely to be weak sisters, and therefore good apparent shorts (but they're fine after the takeover attempt is doomed). Avoid a high short position in a bull market; why buck the trend?

The quality that is desired in a short sale candidate is the ability to subside gracefully, without sudden flareups to annoy and confuse the short seller. Volatility should be fairly low for two months or so before the short sale. However, a volatile past history, followed by a cooling of investor interest, is quite acceptable. After all, there had to be some reason in the past for the stock to rise above its true value. Recent daily volume should be moderate. Occasional high-volume days, especially down days perhaps representing institutional unloading, are quite acceptable.

The stock should already be headed down, and there should be nothing in the fundamentals to indicate any reason for a reversal in the trend. If there is a good number of shares outstanding, if the stock is selling at a relatively high price-earnings ratio, and if the overall market is headed down, the situation is really ripe for selling short. Literally scores of stocks exhibited most or all of the desired characteristics going into the bear market of 1969.

In sum, the gliders, or the shot-down highfliers, are much preferable to the active highfliers as short sale candidates. This is because there is some fundamental logic behind, some factual basis for, the behavior of the gliders, while there is literally no way to predict to what peaks emotional (and perhaps computerized) trading will push a popular stock, nor what the extent of the wild gyrations will be for either the ascent or the descent which will follow.

The article quoted above (with some editing) gave examples of several stocks which conformed to the glider pattern and presented a case history of the decline and fall of Pan American Sulphur Company (now Pasco, Inc.) and Susquehanna, the company which took it over and went down with it.

Risk and Opportunity in Short Selling

The criteria given above for the selection of likely candidates for selling short are sound. They must, of course, be backed up by quantification of risk and opportunity. This can be accomplished with the formulas we have already developed—with one slight but essential modification, the reversal of the algebraic signs between terms.

Risk for longs, you remember, consists of range variability plus the current price factor:

$$\boldsymbol{R_L} = RV + CPF$$

When the current price exceeds the average price, the CPF term is positive to reflect the fact that risk increases along with current price. But when selling short exactly the opposite is true: the higher the current price, the *less* the risk. Therefore, for short sales:

$$\boldsymbol{R_S} = RV - CPF$$

(Of course, when current price is less than average price for a long position, the CPF comes out negative in the basic formula. For a short the sign would still be opposite, that is, positive.)

Similarly for measuring opportunity, a high price for a long position means less opportunity, but for a short it means more, so:

$$\boldsymbol{O}_L = RV - CPF$$
$$\boldsymbol{O}_S = RV + CPF$$

If you are now getting the impression that opportunity for a long is risk for a short, $\boldsymbol{O}_L = \boldsymbol{R}_S$, and risk for a long is opportunity for a short, $\boldsymbol{R}_L = \boldsymbol{O}_S$, you are right on target.

Both longs and shorts can be plotted together on **O/R** diagrams to compare their investment merits and ranked on the same list when computer printouts are used.

Expanded Possibilities for Profit

Expanding the select list to include short sale candidates (which have different selection criteria for quality and so on) does more than double the number of investment opportunities, because weak companies are more numerous than strong ones. Instead of a few "vestal virgins," as the institutional darlings are called, there are hundreds of harlots roaming the Street.

As we have noted, most mutual funds and other institutional investors try to cope with bear markets by going into near-cash securities such as Treasury bills, but it's usually only a token gesture. They may be able to achieve a cash position of 10 percent, but the other 90 percent is going down with the bear market. Even if they were able to go 100 percent cash, they would still be missing the profit potential in selling short. In the nature of things, the big funds couldn't do much short selling, even if their rules allowed them to do it; they have enough trouble selling big blocks long, under present conditions. But that does not mean that short selling is bad; it's simply a constraint under which the big funds must operate, or think they must.

Block Trading

Actually, there is no fundamental reason why large blocks could not be sold, or sold short, under favorable conditions of risk and opportunity near market tops; and there's certainly no problem in buying or covering when prices are severely depressed. (However, if everyone started using risk and opportunity measures which included the current price factor, price swings would become much less severe.)

By way of footnote to the above remarks about block trading, we sometimes wonder just what the main problem is. Are the difficulties exaggerated or is the present market mechanism not functioning well, i.e., failing to bring together potential big buyers and sellers in an efficient way?

Is it possible, we wonder, that they handle these things better in Italy, where the stock exchange is miniscule compared to the NYSE? According to a recent *Fortune* (April 1973), an old friend of ours, Enrico Cuccia, managed to buy controlling interest in that country's largest company, Montedison, without forcing the price up; in fact, prices dropped during the period he was acquiring control. Sr. Cuccia, with whom we have had many enjoyable meetings in Milan, Rome, and Palermo, has long headed Mediobanca, the state-owned investment bank that is one of Italy's most powerful financial institutions.

According to the *Fortune* article ("The Mind-Splitting Job of Running Montedison"):

> The actual buying of Montedison shares was entrusted [by the group seeking control] to Mediobanca's Cuccia, a man who outghosts Cefis [who was installed as president] in keeping out of sight. Cuccia bought up Montedison shares so discreetly that the price of the stock actually declined about fifty points while he was buying.[77]

Normally, as *Fortune* pointed out, a takeover attempt would have resulted in a price increase. Or is that "only in America"?

We do have some contrary evidence. Not long ago we had an appointment with an NYSE specialist, a courtly gentleman whom we had met earlier at his trading post with the help of one of the exchange's governers (a friend of Rosy, to whom this book is dedicated). The appointment, in his office, was for "five minutes after the close" of trading, and we arrived on time, but the specialist was not there. A few minutes passed, and his staff began showing signs of nervousness. "He's always so punctual; he's *never* late," one of the secretaries assured us. Just then he appeared, apologized for his tardiness (six minutes, perhaps), ushered us into his sanctum, and explained the reason for his delay.

Shortly before the close, he told us, a large institutional investor placed a buy order for 500,000 shares of one company for which he was the specialist. He had no matching sell order of that magnitude, naturally, and we can assume (we wish we had asked) that he had nothing like that in his inventory, but he agreed to sell 250,000 shares himself (a large part of which *had* to be short), and he arranged for one of the block houses (Salomon, as we recall) to furnish the rest. All in all, quite a good example of liquidity, we think.

And the price? Only one-quarter point above the last sale. We noted in the next morning's *Wall Street Journal* that the stock led the list of actives for the day. We also noted that the price stayed below that of the closing block transaction for many weeks afterwards, so there was plenty of opportunity to cover any short position at a tidy profit. Let's figure that he cleared only a dollar a share (he doesn't have to pay commissions), or $250,000—not a bad sum for keeping us waiting a few minutes.

It was interesting to hear, during the interview, that he seemed to share a common and ancient prejudice against short-sellers. "None of them build mansions on Fifth Avenue," he said. We admit that we came away with another common prejudice: The specialist is running a wonderful money machine.

15

HEDGE FUND MANAGEMENT

HEDGE FUNDS are out of favor now, but if logic prevails (and the evidence is mixed, as usual, wherever the stock market is concerned) they could well make a comeback when their basic virtues are understood by investors and fund managers. Based upon performance to date, it would seem that the latter are most in need of understanding.

True Portfolio Efficiency Possible

Because it is the only type of investment device which can take full advantage of the profit potential in downward as well as upward price movements, the hedge fund is the ideal vehicle for pursuing true portfolio efficiency. In other words, it is the only one which can maximize overall opportunity in both long and short positions throughout all kinds of markets while minimizing risk.

When the market is "high"—"overpriced" by our measures—much more opportunity is to be found in short positions than in long, which carry much more risk. Conversely, when the market is "low"—"underpriced" or "oversold"—most opportunity lies in long positions, and shorting is very risky indeed. The quantification of risk and opportunity makes possible rational decisions regarding buying and selling at all times, even when emotional or hysterical investors are doing precisely the opposite.

Hedgemanship Paradise Lost

In 1968, when we first became interested in hedge funds during our sojourn at Columbia University's graduate school of business, they were riding very high. Sad to relate, they peaked out, along with the market itself, near the end of that year. Even before *Hedgemanship* was published (in 1970) and the bear market probed its bottom, the hedge funds were in deep trouble. The trouble stemmed from the nearly incredible reason that they had abandoned the very principles which give them their superior profit potential. In the book, we detailed both the basic principles and the ways in which hedge fund managers managed to elude them.

One of our aims in writing *Hedgemanship,* we admit, lay in the hope of raising enough capital to start a new hedge fund, one that would adhere to the valid fundamentals detailed in the book.

In 1968 it would have been easy. That year, if you couldn't find a job when you got out of business school with M.B.A. in hand, you started a hedge fund, and people pressed money upon you. But two years later, the very words "hedge fund" were anathema, and it was another case of "Go Back Where You Stayed Last Night, Baby, I Don't Want You No More."

We did, in fact, get queries from a few big-figured figures, but nothing ever jelled. Partly in sorrow, and partly in an effort to revive interest in hedge funds, we wrote an article for *Barron's* which we called "Hedge Funds Revisited," and which the editor helpfully and more positively retitled "Hedging Does Work: The Technique Is Better Than Some Who Claim to Use It."[63]

Hedging Does Work

Because it still seems like a good summary of what hedge funds are, or should be—and why they turned sour in people's opinion—we'll quote from the article in a moment. (More details can be found in the book *Hedgemanship.*) The article gives emphasis to the pragmatic approach made possible by hedging and minimizes the need for forecasting, saying that it will work well if only the investor keeps in step with the current market. It makes no mention of how the method can be greatly enhanced by risk and opportunity measurement or by the portfolio management techniques described in Chapter 13—subjects to be discussed at the end of this chapter.

The article, somewhat edited, reads:

The hedge fund, an inherently sound investment device, lately has become an object of scorn. Although the Great Shakeout of 1969–70 took the measure of institutional portfolios of all persuasions, hedge funds in general performed worse than the Averages. In consequence, they lost capital and practitioners. Yet, as we shall presently demonstrate, the basic techniques used by hedge funds are not to blame. In nearly every case, the disasters can be traced to an ailment known as inept management.

Hedge funds were "discovered" in 1966 following publication of articles that revealed the truly remarkable capital gains made by two private partnerships managed by A. W. Jones, the field's pioneer. Investment in the wondrous funds exploded in little over two years from $100 million or less scattered over a mere handful of funds to around $2 billion in some 300. For the most part, the money came not from gullible, get-rich-quick small investors but from gullible, get-richer-quick industrialists, bankers, nabobs, economists, and top officers in a number of New York and American Stock Exchange member firms.

Bear Market Blast

As the proliferation approached tulipmania, the funds were hit in 1969 by a bomb subsequently identified as a bear market. The fallout has been contaminating the air ever since. In addition to their dismal performance in the 1969–70 bear market—a period in which they theoretically should have been able to prosper—their troubles were compounded by attacks by the Securities and Exchange Commission charging several leading private hedge funds with fraudulent use of inside information, continued attempts by the commission to extend regulation and disclosure to the private investment partnerships, and massive withdrawals of capital by disgruntled investors.

More recently, an article in *The Wall Street Journal* disclosed that several acknowledged money-wise professionals, including long-time New York Stock Exchange President G. Keith Funston and a group of executives of the First National City Bank's Bahamian subsidiary, got clipped to the tune of several million dollars as a result of their interests in two hedge funds, Takara Partners Ltd. and Armstrong Investors S.A., the managers of which formerly had held top-level positions in prominent Wall Street firms. In this case, the fund managers and others have been charged with a colorful but malodorous assortment of fraud, self-dealing, conflict of interest, and manipulation. While the suits will undoubtedly provide gainful employment for members of the legal profession for years to come, it is perhaps time to step back and take a look at hedge fund techniques, rather than at the way they may have been abused and misused by fund managers.

Definition and Method

For openers, let's clear up the incredible amount of confusion that still exists by defining what we're talking about. A hedge fund is a private or public pool of investment capital which seeks to minimize risk by "hedging" its long positions in some stocks by taking short positions in other stocks, and which usually pursues its goal of maximum capital appreciation by employing leverage to maximize performance.

From this definition it is easy to deduce two reasons for a hedge fund's superior profit potential. One, it can sell short; that is, it can sell borrowed stock in the hope of replacing it later at a lower price. In a bear market—where, again by definition, most stocks are going down—the simple probability of picking a winning short over a winning long is obvious. Two, the use of leverage multiplies performance. If a fund manager is able to make a profit of say 20 percent on unleveraged capital, he should be able to make 40 percent on the same initial capital if he doubles it by using borrowed funds, puts and calls, warrants, or some other form of leverage.

While short selling and leverage are important, they are only two reasons for the hedge fund's superior potential. Also important for the fund manager is the fact that hedging permits a pragmatic approach to investing. An investor need not concern himself with elaborate forecasts based on such inscrutable factors as economic conditions, interest rates, money supply, inflation, war, peace, sunspots, or how he's getting along with his wife. All he need do is keep in tune with the current market by adjusting the proportion of longs and shorts in his portfolio to reflect what the market is doing at any given time.

Since hedging can remove the need for forecasting, any reader with an authenticated record of clairvoyance may stop at this point and go back to counting his money. This article is meant only for fund managers and investors who (1) recognize their own limitations in forecasting and (2) are convinced that stock prices go down as well as up. On that score a quote from John Kenneth Galbraith, which suggests that he may have had first-hand dealing with hedge fund managers, comes to mind. "Financial genius," the professor said, "consists almost entirely of a well-developed capacity for self-delusion combined with a rising market."

In practice, the hedge fund manager tries to select longs which will rise in price and shorts which will fall; if his selection and judgment on the overall trend of the market (as reflected in his ratio of longs to shorts) are good, fund appreciation will result. However, this ideal situation need not be realized completely for the manager to make money. He selects longs which should rise more than the average in a generally rising market and fall less in a declining market. Similarly, he selects shorts which should drop faster than the average in a falling market and rise less in a climbing market. Thus, even if he misjudges the general trend of the market, he is partially sheltered by being in a hedged position.

Of course, if one could really forecast the direction in which the market was heading, he could go 100 percent long, 100 percent short, or take to the sidelines during sideways movements. Unfortunately, bull and bear markets, especially with regard to their duration, tend to be clearly identifiable only after (usually long after) they have ended—when it is too late to serve any practical investment purpose.

The Chicken Market

As a result, we have conceived the idea of the chicken market—one whose future course is unknown. In other words, the market that exists every day. Although the term chicken market may be considered inelegant and even facetious at first glance, it is in fact more useful than the jaded bull and bear labels. It forces the investor into an awareness that he cannot predict the future, and therefore into the realization that the most logical way to invest is by staying attuned to the current market by holding both long and short positions at all times.

We have chosen the chicken as our hero because of its erratic and bird-brained antics. For example, the chicken market may be holding fairly still, roosting, or about to lay an egg; it might be jumping up and down in about the same spot, edging sideways, scratching around, or making clucking noises like those heard in a broker's office; it might be about to run off unpredictably in any direction or actually take to wing.

In all kinds of markets, be they bull, bear, or chicken, the manager of a conventional fund—a mutual fund, for example, or the ordinary investor—attempts to minimize risk by adjusting the relative proportions of stocks (all longs) and cash in his portfolio according to his assessment of the future. By contrast, the hedge fund manager abhors idle cash, stays fully invested in all kinds of markets and attempts to minimize risk by adjusting his ratios of longs and shorts to keep in tune with the current market.

How Managers Failed

The single most important factor in the dismal performance of hedge funds during the 1969–70 bear market was the inability of their managers to select the right shorts. This was a failure of management, not technique. The primary mistake was choosing "highfliers" rather than the much more numerous and dependable laggards which had neither glamor nor bounce. Then, having had their shorts ripped in the early stages of the bear market, the fund managers retreated by going heavily into cash, thus abandoning the other cornerstone of sound hedge fund management, the use of leverage. Such timidity is quite understandable. When you are losing money, leverage magnifies the loss.

Some sense of the confusion that existed even early in the bear market can be gained from a look at the players. The best performing public hedge fund in the first seven months of 1969 was Burger-Kent Special Fund, which declined 14.5 percent in value, compared to an 11.2 percent drop in the Dow Jones Industrials during the same period. In addition to its short exposure to the bear market (it began operations on April 22, 1969), the fund owed much of its "best" rating to the fact that it kept 35–40 percent of its assets in cash equivalents. The maximization of this technique is obviously to put 100 percent of assets into cash and avoid stocks entirely. Yet such a course violates one of the main reasons for the hedge fund's superior profit potential: the use of leverage to stay fully invested at all times.

However, according to *The Wall Street Journal* of August 8, 1969, many other hedge funds, inspired perhaps by the record of Burger-Kent, also were maintaining heavy cash positions. Even some of the pros managing the private hedge funds were "giving cash an increasingly defensive role, letting it run to 50 percent or more of assets," said the *Journal*. The same article reported a pervasive sense of nightmare. Asset losses of as much as 40 percent through July were hitting both private and public hedge funds, compared to an 18 percent drop in the Dow Jones Industrials, causing many managers to abandon both leverage and short selling.

In May 1971, a *Fortune* magazine study of hedge fund asset shrinkage resulting from losses and capital withdrawals during the 21-month period from December 31, 1968, to September 30, 1970, confirmed the worst. Except for Steinhardt, Fine, Berkowitz & Co., which managed to gain 5.1 percent; Lincoln Partners, which lost only 1.2 percent; and Century Partners, whose evaluation was complicated by its ownership of letter stock, capital losses of the 28 funds under study ranged from 36.3 percent to 100 percent. Twenty-one of the 28 were down more than 50 percent. The sole fund which increased its assets profited because it was bearish and therefore heavily short in early 1970.

Assets of the two funds carrying the A. W. Jones label dropped from $120 million to $31 million during the period. Jones, who was caught with shorts which bounced back in the May 1970 upsurge, admits to being out of phase in earlier markets, too. Swept up by the euphoria of the time, he was heavily long in late 1968. Once the market topped and the slide deepened, the Jones portfolio managers cut back their risk by building up short positions, but then it was too little and too late.

These examples underscore the need for an unemotional system for keeping the longs and shorts in a portfolio attuned to the market. Using the basic reasoning that the money value of longs should be proportional to the number of stocks trending upward, and the value of the shorts should be proportional to the number of stocks going down, it is a fairly simple matter to determine the desirable ratios at any given time. Since day-to-day advance and decline figures are too erratic to serve as a practical guide, moving averages must be used. Depending upon the trading inclinations of the investor, the time span of the moving averages can vary from ten days to several months.

Figuring the Ratio

For example, using the Big Board's weekly statistics, it is possible to calculate a series of four-week moving averages for both advances and declines. (The current average is the sum of the latest four weeks' figures for advances, say, divided by four. The average "moves" when the next week's figure becomes available, at which point the figure for five weeks back is dropped.) The desirable percentage of longs in a portfolio at any given time is obtained by dividing the moving average for advances by the sum of the advance and decline moving averages. To illustrate, if the advance average is 900 and the decline 600, the desirable long percentage is 60, and the balance, or 40 percent of the value of the portfolio, should be invested in shorts.

It is instructive to follow how such a guideline might have helped hedge fund managers from late 1968 through the 1969–70 bear market and into the present. Our method of setting the proportion of longs to shorts indicates a ratio of 48 percent longs to 52 percent shorts going into November 1968, a peak of 65/35 on the 28th (the day the NYSE Composite Index topped at 61.27), and a rapid falloff to 36/64 on January 8, 1969 (a day before the Composite bottomed at 56.77). Throughout the ups and downs of 1969, the long/short ratio varied between 21/79 and 64/36, while the Index ranged between a high of 59.32 and a low of 49.31. The ratio generally topped and bottomed along with or before the Index.

The same general pattern held true throughout 1970, as the market hit its low of 36.79 on May 24 and staggered upward to the 50-level by year's end. The long/short ratio bottomed at 19/81 on May 22 and shot up to 54/46 four weeks later, then dropped off with the reaction. The long/short ratio reached a high of 72.5/27.5 on September 11, dropped to 36.5/63.5 on November 30 (more than two weeks before the NYSE Composite hit a temporary low of 45.00), then climbed to 69/31 by December 18.

The selective nature of the early 1971 bull market was indicated by the early divergence of the Composite and the long/short ratio. The Index climbed from the 50-level to a high of 57.76 on April 28, then fell to a low of 51.66 on August 9 and 10. Our long/short ratio peaked on January 22, then subsided, but kept the longs in the majority as the Index moved upward. An intermediate peak of 56/44 was hit on April 23 (a week before the Index topped out), then dipped rapidly to 34/66 on May 28. The ratio of longs to shorts hit a low of 32/68 as the market bottomed in August, then climbed to 68/32 just before the Index topped at 56.04.

Although our long/short ratio usually tops and bottoms with, or in advance of, the market averages, no claims are made for the predictive powers of the system. They are not necessary. The pragmatic approach of hedgemanship requires only keeping in tune with the current market. Using this system, it is impossible to miss market turns, as so many of the pros have done. Both the market and our long/short ratio bottomed in late May 1970, but for months thereafter professional money managers and stock market commentators alike were asking: Is the bear market over?

Many are still wondering.

Adjusting the Ratio for Risk and Opportunity

Although the method of allocating funds to long and short positions by the use of a ratio of moving averages of advances and declines is a very useful one for keeping in step with the market, the article quoted above did not explain how it could be given a forward-looking stance through the use of risk and opportunity measures.

A method of "adjusting" dollars for risk is demonstrated in *Hedgemanship*. It consists of weighting the current dollar value of each stock in a portfolio by its risk value, totaling the longs and the shorts, and determining the long/short ratio. This "adjusted dollar" ratio is the one which should keep in step with the moving advance/decline ratio.

It is even easier to use opportunity for the longs and shorts. To demonstrate with some figures from the *Barron's* article:

The unadjusted L/S ratio when the market peaked out in late November 1968 was 65/35. Now, suppose we were still holding some longs into the high-risk area, so that their opportunity averaged only 0.2; and suppose that the average opportunity of the shorts at these high prices was 0.8. Weighting each by opportunity, the adjusted L/S ratio is $(65 \times 0.2)/(35 \times 0.8) = 33/67$. In other words, as the market peaked, only 33 percent of the money was in longs, and 67 percent in shorts, ready for the roller coaster. This situation at the peak naturally implies the liquidation of high-risk stocks as the market approached the peak, and the concurrent accumulation of high-opportunity shorts.

At the bear market lows of May 1971, the unadjusted L/S ratio was 32/68. Let's say that the few shorts we had not taken profits on and still held averaged only 0.1 in opportunity, while the longs were at 0.9. At the market bottom, then, the opportunity-weighted ratio was 81/19, so 81 percent of the portfolio investment was in long positions, poised for the advance.

In practice, it is doubtful if any stock with as little opportunity as 0.1 would be held; but it would depend upon the guidelines set in the portfolio management program described in Chapter 13. The approach outlined above is a good one to use in conjunction with, and as a check on, that program when it is applied to a hedge fund.

In conclusion, we wrote *Hedgemanship* with the firm belief that the hedge fund is an inherently superior investment vehicle. We still think so.

16

THE BASIC FALLACIES OF MODERN CAPITAL MARKET THEORY

NOW THAT WE have explained the elements of our quantitative system, and their application to a practical system of portfolio management, we can give further attention to the approach which is in many fundamental ways at variance with ours—that of the modern capital market theorists.

In the introductory chapter we gave a very brief summary of the theory, and its implications for portfolio management, along with the admittedly unrealistic assumptions underlying the theory. It doesn't matter that the assumptions are absurd, say the modcaps; all that matters is whether the model works. At various places throughout the text, we have tested their working model against the real market and found it lacking. It was not an exhaustive test, so now we'll let them present their case in more detail, quoting from their own writings, as we continue our testing.

We are aware that, in attempting to expose what we believe to be the fallacies of modern capital market theory, we are going up against a large body of opinion that is cherished and defended by academically oriented thinkers and researchers, including top professors in highly rated graduate schools, who have won the backing of the Securities and Exchange Commission, the Bank Administration Institute, and many prestigious, profit-oriented financial institutions.

We are also aware, and we have demonstrated, that any questioning of the established modcap dogma can arouse intense feelings in the breasts of those who embrace it. Our object, as we have pointed out, does not lie in the need for enemies, but rather in the fact that the theory has gained such momentum that we believe it should be challenged.

Developments are coming in fast. The random-walk theory has just made the front page of *The Wall Street Journal,*[36] along with the news that money is actually being managed on modcap principles, in "market index funds," which seek only to match the performance of a market index. The Wells Fargo Bank of San Francisco "is currently marketing through private placement a $100 million closed-end fund for pension money, called the Stagecoach Fund," which will invest in all the stocks of the S & P 500 index. Batterymarch Financial Management Corporation of Boston will also seek to match the performance of the same index. The American National and Harris banks of Chicago have already "restructured billions of dollars in their corporate and personal trust accounts to somewhat mirror the composition of the S & P 500," and American Express Investment Management "is considering starting a new fund for the small investor" that would try to duplicate the performance of some unspecified NYSE index (we would guess the industrial, which is more volatile than the composite).

As if the above were not enough shocking news, Benjamin Graham, the very pillar of fundamentalism, is beginning to make sounds like a modcap. In the latest edition of *The Intelligent Investor,* he says, "the current price of each . . . stock pretty well reflects the salient factors in its financial record plus the general opinion as to its future prospects."[26] We can stand having economist Paul Samuelson, the recent Nobel laureate, in the opposite camp (he has "proven rigorously that independence of successive price changes is consistent with an efficient market").[42] But *Benjamin Graham!*

For the reader who may think we could be exaggerating our alarm over the management of funds along the lines laid down by modern capital market theorists, we can review the implications by quoting from Michael C. Jensen's "Risk, the Pricing of Capital Assets, and the Evaluation of Investment Portfolios":[32]

1) Minimize management expenses and brokerage commissions. That is, a buy-and-hold policy should be followed as closely as possible. [In

other words, abandon stock analysis, any thought that you can beat the market, any trading at favorable price levels; and your brains.]

2) Concentrate on the maintenance of a perfectly diversified portfolio [one which will move up and down in lock-step with the market, no more and no less; if you can't beat the market, join it].

3) Maintain a constant level of systematic risk [beta] as closely as possible. A fund which establishes a risk level and attracts investors on this basis should avoid sudden shifts in its risk [variability] level, since unexpected changes . . . are likely to leave investors with inappropriate portfolios. [Here, the delusion seems to be that investors are more interested in a constant rate of pleasant and unpleasant surprises than in the manager's trying to take advantage of price changes in individual stocks.]

It is obvious from our parenthetical remarks that we do find the implications alarming.

We don't intend here a full critique of modern capital market theory, nor do we intend to teach the theory itself, for we're something less than a True Believer, as our comments throughout the text have indicated. (A short course on the subject may be had by reading relevant parts of the glossary, starting with Capital Asset Pricing Model.)

Readings

Readers who want to know more about the theory—and it is an interesting one—are referred to the Bibliography. A good summary is to be found in "The Efficient Market Model,"[69] by Oldrich A. Vasicek and John A. McQuown, an article that appeared in the September 1972 issue of the *Financial Analysts Journal.* (The *Journal* is itself an excellent and generally readable publication that has done much to introduce some degree of logic into the investment decision-making process.)

A more extended treatment of the theory, and one which is able to devote more space to its theoretical origins and backing, is a book that appeared while we were still writing ours, and which we recommend to interested readers, even though we disagree with most of it. The book is *The Stock Market: Theories and Evidence,* by James H. Lorie and Mary T. Hamilton. We do not wish to slight the lady professor (who, in the nature of things, probably did most of the work on the book), but Lorie's is the big name among modern capital market theorists. Professor of business administration at the University of Chicago's graduate school, he is director of its Center for Research in Security Prices (sponsored by Merrill Lynch, no less), and it was he who served as chairman of the advisory committee to the Bank Administration Institute in its efforts, mentioned elsewhere in the present work, to devise a system for measuring the investment performance of pension (and other) funds. The Lorie and Hamilton opus can be regarded as both authoritative and the latest word on the subject of modern capital market theory. As such, we quote it from time to time.

Origins

Modern capital market theory is derived in large part from the works of Harry M. Markowitz (the Grandfather of Beta) and William F. Sharpe (the Father of Beta), both of whom, in spite of the degree of superannuation implied in their titles, are very much alive and kicking. The Grandfather, at last report, was running some arbitrage money, which required little or no use of beta. We find this significant, and also Markowitz' statement to the *Institutional Investor,* "My book was really a closed logical piece. . . . I'd really said all I wanted to, and it was time to go on to something else."[72] This offhand dismissal of the Old Testament of the modern capital market theorists should give them pause.

The Father, Sharpe, now with Stanford University Business School and consulting for Merrill Lynch, continues to write articles on risk and portfolio theory, some of which we have occasion to refer to, along with the works of the now numerous progeny. We regret that we cannot here give balanced and comprehensive credit to all who have contributed to the subject.

However, in fairness to a few prophets now almost lost in the mists of modcap history, we should perhaps mention Louis Bachelier, who in *Nature* back in 1905 showed that commodity speculation in France was a "fair game" which neither buyer nor seller could expect to win; Osborne, noted earlier, who compared the stock market to Brownian motion and gave further support to the random-walk theory; and Von Neuman and Morgenstern, whose *Theory of Games and Economic Behavior* has been credited with inspiring Markowitz.

Markowitz' renowned contribution to capital market theory was the "efficient portfolio." His mathematical portfolio model, unusable for all practical purposes in the form in which he presented it because of the great number of inputs required and the impossibility of obtaining them in any case from any known source, can nevertheless be expressed quite simply in words:

An efficient portfolio is one with the highest expected return for a given level of risk or, conversely, one with the lowest risk for a given expected return. The idea itself, of course, is not new. Many money managers have pursued the idea of an efficient portfolio, even though they might have been hard pressed to define one, let alone write a formula to express it.

Here, then, is one of the few points on which we can agree with the modcaps, and here also the agreement with Markowitz ends. We do not agree with his definition of risk, nor his measurement of it by variance in return, nor any other measures of variability—all of which are only partial measures of risk—and we have serious doubts that his "expected return" has much practical significance.

Father Sharpe performed a commendable service when he conceived a simplified version of the Markowitz model. His simplified model eliminated the need to estimate the covariance of each stock with every other stock by substituting the covariance of each with the market, thereby reducing the number of required "probabilistic estimates of future performances of securities" (meaning expected returns and covariances) from 5,150 to 302 for analyzing 100 securities, and from 2,003,000 to 6,002 for analyzing 2,000.[56] This news must have brought audible sighs of relief from the computers involved.

However, Sharpe's so-called diagonal model is, like that of Markowitz, a static one, because it makes no allowance for dynamic portfolio changes due to shifting composition and current price.

So much for background. As for the theory itself, the highlights (following Vasicek and McQuown) are summarized in the Glossary under the heading "Capital Asset Pricing Model." Their paper, titled "The Efficient Market Model," already noted, begins by warning that "the authors are attempting to expose the basics of capital market theory and not to validate it per se." (The alert reader will note that their use of the verb *to expose* differs somewhat from ours.) The content of the paper, nonetheless, gives abundant testimony to their warm espousal of the cause—and McQuown, in fact, heads the Wells Fargo Stagecoach Fund, already mentioned.

Definition

The definition of capital market theory, like the modcaps' definition of risk itself, is somewhat blurred. In the literature, the terms *capital market theory* (usually preceded by *modern*), *capital asset pricing model, efficient market model,* and even *beta theory* and the *random-walk theory* are often used as though they were interchangeable.

The Glossary regards capital market theory as the broad term which encompasses all the others—that is, all of the theory and models stemming from the works of Markowitz, Sharpe, and their disciples. The efficient market model (or theory) and the capital asset pricing model are synonymous for all practical purposes, although Vasicek and McQuown call the latter "the most significant part of" the former. Beta (market-related variability), as well as alpha (variability not related to market movements), are factors in the equations describing the theorists' market models. Finally, the random-walk theory, whose validity is based on not very convincing empirical studies, is used to shore up capital market theory on the practical side. The latter theory, developed during efforts to explain the supposedly random nature of stock market price changes, was parent to the broader body of theory.

It is not our purpose here to criticize the mathematics of capital market theory in detail, but simply to point out what we consider to be the theory's most unrealistic bases and conclusions.

Starting with Risk

At the very base of the shaky foundation of modern capital market theory is the theorists' imprecise and misleading definition of risk. That is why we dwelt upon the subject at such length in Chapter 2. The importance of risk could hardly be overstated, but it should not be equated with uncertainty, a much broader term which includes opportunity as well. (Just because a group of cultists agree among themselves to call succotash "beans" does not alter the fact that the mess also contains a lot of corn.)

However, having decided that risk is uncertainty, the wrong conclusions seem bound to follow, namely (1) risk can be measured by variability, (2) a higher return will result from assuming greater risk, (3) the market is an efficient one in which stocks are priced correctly at all times, and (4) it is impossible to beat the market over time (except perhaps by using leverage or inside information).

Let's examine these conclusions as they are stated in the theorists' own writings, relying heavily on Vasicek and McQuown, Lorie and Hamilton, and such authoritative sources as the Bank Administration Institute and the Securities and Exchange Commission, both of which tapped top academic talent to write their reports. In other words, we'll let these experts "expose" themselves (using that term in the same sense that Vasicek and McQuown have used it in their paper).

We have already discussed the modcaps' definition of risk. Now let's look at the four major dubious conclusions stemming from it.

17

CAN RISK BE MEASURED BY VARIABILITY?

THE BANK ADMINISTRATION INSTITUTE'S Advisory Committee, headed by James Lorie, in its final recommendations relating to risk, declared that it was in favor of estimating "the degree of risk actually assumed by a fund manager by measuring the variability from period to period in the fund's time-weighted rate of return," and it chose "the use of the mean absolute deviation as the best measure of variability."

Mean Absolute Deviation

Mean absolute deviation is easy to calculate; it is simply the sum of the absolute differences between each observation divided by the number of observations. ("Absolute" differences means that plus and minus signs are ignored when they are summed.) The BAI study illustrated the mechanics of calculation by a theoretical example:

First the average rate of return is determined:

Period	*Actual Return*
1	– 2%
2	10
3	20
4	– 8
	20%
Average Rate of Return	5%

Then absolute deviations and the mean are determined:

Period	*Actual Return*	*Average Return*	*Absolute Deviation*
1.	– 2%	5%	– 7%
2.	10	5	5
3.	20	5	15
4.	– 8	5	–13
Total Deviation.			40%
Mean Absolute Deviation from the Average Rate of Return			10%

Now, using the BAI method, let's calculate the risk of another fund, one whose manager succeeds in gaining a steady 5 percent per period:

Period	*Actual Return*	*Average Return*	*Absolute Deviation*
1.	+5%	+5%	0%
2.	+5%	+5%	0
3.	+5	+5	0
4.	+5	+5	0
Mean Absolute Deviation			0%

So far, so good; the return is steadier so the risk is lower: 0 percent compared to 10 percent in the first example.

But suppose a fund manager *loses* money at a steady rate, say 5 percent a period? Using the BAI method, his risk would be:

Period	*Actual Return*	*Average Return*	*Absolute Deviation*
1.	–5%	–5%	0%
2.	–5	–5	0
3.	–5	–5	0
4.	–5	–5	0
Mean Absolute Deviation			0%

So it appears that all funds, no matter whether they are making money or losing money (and no matter how fast or how slowly) have no risk at all—as long as they are gaining or losing at a steady clip!

We have used an extreme case, perhaps, so let's return to the BAI's own example, only reversing the signs on actual returns:

Period	*Actual Return*	*Average Return*	*Absolute Deviation*
1.	+ 2%	−5%	+ 7%
2.	−10	−5	− 5
3.	−20	−5	−15
4.	+ 8	−5	+13
Total Deviation.			40%
Mean Absolute Deviation			10%

So, a fund losing, on average, 5 percent per period has the same mean absolute deviation—which the BAI equates with risk—as another fund that is *gaining,* on average, 5 percent per period.

Perhaps we can now generalize, formulating what we call the *Bank Administration Institute Risk Rule:* It does not matter whether a fund is making money or losing money, its risk is the same as that of all other funds either making or losing money at the same average rate.

In his paper questioning the BAI approach, Lemont K. Richardson does a good job of exposing and summing up "the inability of these techniques [based upon variability standards as measures of risk] to differentiate meaningfully among the degrees of investment risk attaching to growth companies, stable industry companies, and declining industry companies."[50] Or *any* companies, we would add.

Standard Deviation

Another popular measure of risk to be found among the voluminous literature on the subject (and we confess we've read only a fraction of it) is *standard deviation*—a common and useful statistical measure of dispersion. The standard deviation of any set of numbers (or "observations") is calculated by summing the squares of the differences of each observation from their mean, dividing by the number of observations, and obtaining the square root of the result. It is usually designated by the letter s, or sigma, σ. (To be exact, s is used for the standard deviation of a *sample* and σ for that of a *population* from which the sample is drawn. Now aren't you sorry you asked?)

$$s = \sqrt{\frac{\Sigma(X - \bar{X})^2}{n}}$$

where X = a single observation, $\bar{X}$ = the mean of all observations, and n = the number of observations.

Sharpe, in a recent article already referred to, "Risk, Market Sensitivity and Diversification," writes: "This paper used standard statistical measures of variation to represent risk. The risk of a security is measured by standard deviation,"[58] which he, like almost all risk theorists defines as the standard deviation of the rate of return, or the percentage price change plus yield. He then goes on to break down risk into two components, market and nonmarket risk. Let's look at the appropriateness of using standard deviation as a measure of any kind of risk.

Using the BAI example cited earlier (and it is instructive to follow the details of calculation), the standard deviation:

$$s = \sqrt{\frac{-7^2 + 5^2 + 15^2 + -13^2}{4}}$$

$$= \sqrt{\frac{49 + 25 + 225 + 169}{4}}$$

$$= \sqrt{117} = 10.8$$

Let's pass quickly over the propriety of giving the deviation of 15 a weight 9 times that of the deviation of 5 (because of squaring them) and look at the squaring process itself. A squared number, even a negative one, is always positive. Therefore, reversing all signs, i.e., assuming losses for gains and vice versa—as we did in the previous example—will result in exactly the same standard deviation.

Back to the BAI Risk Rule: It does not matter whether you win or lose; it's by whose rules you play the game.

Variance and Covariance

Vasicek and McQuown, and many others from Markowitz on down, use *variance* and *covariance* as measures of risk. Variance is obtained in the same way as standard deviation, except that the final step—taking the square root—is omitted. Variance, in other words, is the square of standard deviation and is equal to 117 in our numerical example.

As Vasicek and McQuown use it, variance is "the mean squared deviation of the distribution of future returns from the expected value," the expected rate of return being "the mean value of the distribution of future returns," or "the value around which future returns are expected to center."

Covariance between two rates of return is defined as "the mean value of the product of the deviations of the two rates from their expected values." Unlike the measures discussed earlier, which are always positive, covariance can be either positive or negative, depending upon whether the rates move in the same or opposite direction. A few stocks, such as gold mining issues, tend to move against the market averages.

Both variance and covariance, like mean absolute deviation and standard deviation, are simply measures of variability—not total risk—and should not be equated with it, since they share the same shortcomings.

Markowitz, it seems, was the first to apply the concept of covariance to stock behavior, and his followers have striven to give it practical application ever since. Covariance with the market, introduced by Sharpe, is the basis upon which beta theory rests, and even the SEC—usually considered to be a hard-headed, pragmatic outfit—has embraced beta.

Institutional Investor Study Report of the SEC

More recent than the BAI study—and presumably even more authoritative, since it carries the imprimatur of the government agency which regulates the investment industry—is the SEC *Study Report.*[54] The report terms beta a volatility measure (not the best use of the term volatility, as we have demonstrated) and—after some hemming and hawing—says that risk and volatility are used "virtually interchangeably" in their report. As a basic step in its performance measurement procedure (which it uses to calculate "risk-adjusted performance"), the report calculates what it calls a "relative volatility coefficient," which is the ratio of portfolio or fund return to market return—after first deducting from each the Treasury bill rate. When a series of such coefficients is regressed mathematically or plotted graphically, the slope of the "best-fitting" straight line through the data points is a measure of the average volatility of the fund during the period observed.

It all sounds complicated, and it is. And what do they wind up with? Once again, the measure of risk is merely one of variability in rate of return, with the same shortcomings as those already reviewed.

Variability Should Be Used, Not Shunned

Although the SEC, according to the report mentioned, would like to penalize fund managers for investing in volatile stocks and also for turnover, both of these—when used properly—are laudable and proper means of portfolio management.

In up markets, according to the modcaps' own dogma, the stocks with high betas will gain the most. In down markets, of course, they will lose the most—but this is precisely when the capable fund manager should be out of such stocks (or selling them short). But moving in and out, even at appropriate times, means turnover—and that is always naughty, it would seem.

The SEC, along with the BAI and modcaps in general, have not considered *real* risk, based on current price at the time of purchase and sale. Even a highly volatile stock, as we have seen, can be bought at a price where the risk is measurably low, and doing so would constitute good portfolio management, even if it were sold a few months later after a 50 percent gain.

If performance is to be adjusted for risk, it should be on the basis of real risk, not simply variability in rate of return. Specifically, it should be based upon what happened to the stock after it was purchased for the portfolio. Buying a high-volatility stock which increases in value obviously shows better management judgment than buying a low-volatility stock which declines in value (always provided the former in sold at an appropriate time to capture the price appreciation).

But the modcaps' theory is a static one. It assumes buying and holding, riding the market up and down, taking neither profits nor defensive measures. Their static theory has led them inevitably to their static portfolio policy.

Rate of Return

What the modcaps call "rate of return" itself has weaknesses as a measure of performance. It varies in value along with the arbitrary time periods selected to measure it. It is nobody's real rate of return, unless he happens to buy and sell on the dates selected by the statistical analyst—a most unlikely coincidence. And it doesn't even measure real variability of total wealth, because it doesn't recognize the variability which takes place *between* the terminal dates (as does range variability).

"The greatest advantage of the average yield approach is that it permits the standard deviation, a measurement of the dispersion of the annual yields [or those for any other time period], to be computed."[61] So writes Robert M. Soldofsky in *Financial Analysts Journal,* a publication which does not often indulge in humor.

We believe that Soldofsky has identified "the greatest advantage" to the modcaps of all the variability measures, but we're more in tune with Richardson, when he writes, "Measuring investment risk in terms of variability . . . is a highly arbitrary and misleading concept and is subject to a number of serious technical flaws."[50]

(As we have already noted, measures of dispersion can be applied to our range variabilities as well as to rates of return.)

Summary

The intent of this chapter was to answer the question, "Can Risk Be Measured by Variability?"—as one of the basic fallacies of modern capital market theory says it can. If any reader is unable to answer firmly in the negative, we suggest: Go back and reread the chapter.

18

CAN INVESTORS DEMAND RETURNS?

In a passage quoted earlier, Robert A. Levy writes: "Available evidence indicates that common stock investors demand and receive a higher level of return with increased variability."[37] This is a concise and well-stated version of:

The Well-Known Proposition

Randall A. Robinson, research director for the Bank Administration Institute, puts it more traditionally:

> One of the most extensively documented propositions in the field of finance is that people can enjoy, on the average, a higher rate of return by assuming more risk . . . . No serious research on the subject, covering extended periods of time, controverts the proposition. Many different definitions of risk and return were used in the studies.[51]

The first sentence appears so often, almost unchanged, in writings by the True Believers that one is tempted by the thought that they convene regularly, like members of some monkish order, to chant it in unison. Perhaps they do need some such method to bolster their faith, for the evidence (even their own) is underwhelming.

The chant makes it appear that superior investment results are so readily accomplished. According to W. H. Wagner and S. C. Lau (who are associated with the Wells Fargo Bank management services department), "Above average returns can easily be generated for those investors willing to undertake above average risks."[70] Their study, which opened with the ritual statement, "Recent advances in economic theory emphasize that investors who hold portfolios of riskier stocks should expect higher returns than more conservative investors," examined the relationship between risk and return of theoretical portfolios whose degree of riskiness was based upon Standard and Poor's ratings of stock quality.

The periods studied were June 1960 to May 1965 and (overlapping) June 1960 to June 1970, and—sure enough—they found that "returns increase as additional risk is undertaken," or "as the quality [their risk indicator] of the individual issues declines."

Selective Empirical Techniques

We think it significant that:

> The five-year period 1965–70 was not studied. Because there was virtually no net change in market level during that period, it cannot be used to illustrate the normal difference in return expected between high- and low-risk portfolios.

Here we observe a fine example of selective empirical technique, i.e., playing down or discarding data which might weaken or annihilate the theory that one has set out to bolster.

The five-year period thrown out because it would not substantiate the "normal" relationship between risk and return, was not, as stated, one of "virtually no net change in market level," as we eyeball the figures on the charts. Over that period the NYSE composite index suffered a net *drop* of about 14 percent, the S & P 500 some 13 percent, and the Dow Jones Industrials about (or should we say "virtually"?) 29 percent. In contrast, the periods studied in support of their well-known proposition showed net *rises* of about 57 percent and 38 percent in the S & P 500.

To their credit, because it does not support their thesis, Wagner and Lau finally come around to admitting that:

> Of course, there are periods in which the actual returns do not fulfill investors' expectation of extra return for bearing systematic [market-

related] risk. In fact, the period 1965–70 provides an example. Before the fact, however, an investor can always expect higher returns for bearing higher systematic risk.

We don't wish to go into detail here on the inconclusive nature of other empirical studies, which often stubbornly refuse to back a neat relationship between risk (by which the theorists mean variability) and return. (Interested readers can find contrary evidence in the writings of such proponents as Lorie and Hamilton[40] and the SEC *Study Report*[54] and in the critical article by Richardson.[50])

Expected Return

The quotations we have given from Wagner and Lau are additional evidence of the tricky nature of the concept of expected return, one of the basics of modern capital market theory—from Markowitz on down the line.

Expected return is a perfectly valid and useful concept in statistical analysis, where it is based upon weighting various possible outcomes by their probabilities of occurrence. The concept gets a bit hairy, though, when the modcaps apply it to stock pricing. Let's suppose that a stock opens at 50 and drops (or rises) five points by the day's close. Do the modcaps really believe that all of their so-called rational investors have recalculated their expected returns during a few hours so as to reflect precisely the 10 percent change in price? For us, the boggle coefficient approaches infinity.

Moreover, herein lies one of the big contradictions of modern capital market theory. Let's suppose that the 10 percent price change was not due to any new information about the company concerned, but simply a perfect beta-correlation with the movement of the market itself. Did expected returns from the company really drop (or rise) 10 percent during the day? Again, $BC \rightarrow \infty$.

Actually, it is not necessary to resort to formal statistical concepts in order to understand the fact that anyone betting on a long shot *expects* a higher payoff *if he hits.* Of course he does—and he did so long before Markowitz. But he knows that the odds are against him, so he may be *expecting in vain.* Modcaps, however, treat expected return ambivalently as (1) a sure thing and (2) something fleeting, changing with the mood of the market.

Yet Another Inconsistency

Another great inconsistency lies in the gap between the modcaps' claim that it is easy to obtain higher returns simply by investing in riskier stocks, and their equally firm belief that no other portfolio can beat the market portfolio over time.

We must always keep in mind that when the modcaps say "risk" they are really talking about variability, which is only one factor in real risk—the other factor being current price. It should be obvious that a highly volatile stock, purchased near its expected high, can have a much lower expected return than a less volatile stock bought near its expected low.

Richardson twits the modcaps' version of risk:

> The risk-reward proposition endorsed by the BAI study and others that investors, on average, can realize higher returns by taking higher risks suggests that investors tend to get what they expect or that expected and realized return are identical . . . and common stock investors who bought at the top of the market when the risks were greatest would, on average, do better than those who dollar averaged.[50]

He quotes Walter A. Morton: "If investors always get what they expect, then all risk and uncertainty would go out the window."[46]

Both Richardson and Morton, of course, are using risk in its true sense, not that of the modcaps. We got in a twit or two of our own in the "Beta Mousetrap" article in *Barron's:*

> Even the earliest risk researchers pointed out the correlation between yield and risk (as expressed by bond ratings) and came to the general conclusion that lower-rated bonds yielded the highest rates of return because investors *demanded* higher rates to compensate for the higher risks. Following this line of reasoning, and backing it up with both theoretical and statistical studies, most researchers concluded that the riskier the security, the higher, on average, the rate of return. (Herein may lie the reason why the Greater Fool Theory works so well in practice; if profitability increases with risk, it follows that the riskier the deal, the more the next sucker should be willing to pay for it.)[62]

An Alternate Version

With the knowledge that the modcaps really mean variability when they talk about risk, and noting some of the reasons for inconsistencies in the empirical studies, is it possible to come up with some version of their risk-reward credo that we can live with?

Our suggestion, based upon our risk and opportunity approach as well as a review of some statistical studies:

(1) Investors can, on average, realize a higher rate of return by investing in higher volatility issues, bought at average price and held during a period of generally rising prices. (2) If held during a period of generally falling prices, precisely the opposite result will occur. (3) In the first case, if purchases are made at prices below average, and sales above, an even higher rate of return will result. (4) In the second case, if purchases are made at prices above average, and sales below, an even lower return will result.

To generalize: High-volatility stocks carry the greatest potentials for both gain and loss, but overall market movements and buying and selling prices are also important, because they can add to, or detract from, both potentials.

In fact, the only justification for the modcaps' version of the risk-return relationship lies in the very long-term upward trend of the market—which is really not a very useful phenomenon for portfolio management. How would a policy of investing in the highfliers of 1929 have paid off in the long run? Many of them took decades to recover, and some even went out of business before the market regained 1929 levels. Investing in the averages would not have been wise, either.

More Contrary Evidence

Any version of the risk-return relationship can be upset by the supply and demand factors in the market. For example, the current (June 1973) issue of *Fortune,* reporting on "The Strange News about Risk and Return," compares the stocks in the magazine's "First 500" companies with those in the "Second 500," and concludes that "Wall Street may have to take another look at those beta coefficients."[25] For 1972, the beta relationship was just the reverse of the one expected—the second 500 (with relatively high betas) showing lower returns than the first 500, even in the generally rising market.

The explanation, no doubt, lay in the developing "two-tier" market dominated by the large institutions, which were concentrating on the biggies and neglecting the others. In this specific case, hopefully of limited duration, it would seem to be true that institutional investors, by acting in unison, can demand, and get, higher returns even from *less* risky stocks (but wait until they try to cash in their chips!).

Great Expectations

The question this chapter set out to answer is this: Can investors demand, or even *expect* with any degree of confidence, to receive higher returns by assuming higher risk? The answer is clearly "no." Especially if we are talking about *real* risk, as opposed to variability, the answer is "no—quite the opposite."

In sum, the second great fallacy of modern capital market theory can be answered by what we call "Dickens' Law of Expectations": Expect in vain; demand and be damned!

19

WHICH RANDOM WALK? WHAT EFFICIENT MARKET?

ONE OF THE DIFFICULTIES faced by the critic of the random-walk theory, out of which modern capital market theory evolved, and upon which the whole theory still rests, is deciding with *which* of the many versions extant to come to grips.

Artists and Models

James H. Lorie and Mary T. Hamilton offer the commonest "three forms of the efficient market (formerly, the random-walk) hypothesis: (1) the weak form; (2) the semistrong form; and (3) the strong form."[42]

Charles P. Jones, and others before him, have described the "broad random walk," as opposed to the "basic random walk."[34]

And John Michael Murphy invokes the "grand" version in justification for his analysis of "The Value Line Contest: 1969."[47] (Presumably the alternatives to "grand" are "petit," "shabby," or maybe "upright.") Comes now James W. Wetzler, a Harvard graduate student, who wrote in the *Financial Analysts Journal,* in which Murphy's piece appeared, that the evidence presented by Murphy "is not relevant to the random-walk hypothesis."[73]

C. W. J. Granger, a British statistician and econometrician, in a valiant effort to set everyone straight, delivered himself of a paper titled "What the Random Walk Model Does NOT Say"[28] (emphasis emphatically his). Sticking strictly to his thesis, the University of NOTtingham professor never states exactly what his own version of the random-walk model DOES say, but he makes it very clear that the theory is about *absolute* prices, and it says nothing whatever about *relative* price movement.

Granger says that "the question of whether a randomly selected portfolio does as well as portfolios actually selected by financial analysts . . . *has nothing to do with random walks*." Analysts, he says, may be able to anticipate news specific to a stock, hence anticipate *relative* price movements, even though market movements affecting the *absolute* level of stock prices may be a strict random walk. He therefore has words of cheer for the old-hat stock analysts whom the modcaps have declared obsolete: "It is possible to choose a portfolio that performs better than either some randomly chosen portfolio or some market average or index."

He follows with the sensible disclaimer: "Whether or not the actual *performance* of the average analyst is satisfactory is another matter."

Widespread Misunderstanding

As to why there has been so much misunderstanding of the random-walk model, Granger states: "The truth is . . . that most adverse criticism is by writers who have clearly not read the original paper and so have become familiar with the model only through a number of popular, non-technical accounts which have been sometimes misleading."

Here Granger underreaches, for the misunderstanding is not confined to critics, but is at least as prevalent among those who have warmly embraced random walk, including those who presumably have done the required reading.

Consider, for example, Lorie and Hamilton's "three forms" of the efficient market hypothesis (formerly, in their words, the random walk). As the forms increase from "weak" to "strong," they actually *decrease* in credibility (if we go along with Granger—which we do). According to Lorie and Hamilton:

> The weak form asserts that current prices fully reflect the information implied by the historical sequence of prices. In other words, an investor cannot enhance his ability to select stocks by knowing the history of successive prices, and the results of analyzing them in all possible ways.

This weak form comes closest to agreement with Granger, although he might well ask the authors to define "reflect" and "implied." If the weak form says that the chartists can't produce superior results, we can agree.

Contradictions

Here we see further evidence of one of the apparent contradictions of modern capital market theory. The modcaps analyze historical prices to obtain their betas (measures of co-movement with the market), which they insist can be projected into the future (this is where their "leap of faith" is required), and they say that superior returns can be obtained by investing in stocks with higher betas. If even the weak form is true, then beta, at the very foundation of the theory, is on shaky ground.

Turning to another form of the theory, according to Lorie and Hamilton:

> The semistrong form of the hypothesis asserts that current prices fully reflect public knowledge about the underlying companies, and that efforts to acquire and analyze this knowledge cannot be expected to produce superior investment results.

This form is clearly contrary to Granger's assertion that it *is* possible to anticipate *relative* price movements and thereby produce superior results.

Finally, we arrive at the very pinnacle of "strength":

> The strong form asserts that not even those with privileged information can often make use of it to secure superior investment results.

This form, like the previous one, is also contrary to Granger—only more so. In any case, the qualifying word "often" vitiates the definition of the strong form. Besides its indefiniteness, it carries legal undertones. Inside information can be very profitable, as it was in the Merrill Lynch–Douglas Aircraft case,[63] for example. Although the resultant investigation led to an intense round of wrist-slapping by the SEC, it certainly did not put a stop to similar hanky-panky. If the strong form were valid, of course, the commission could abandon its costly efforts to police insider trading. There would seem to be a dichotomy within the commission itself, for its *Institutional Investor Study Report* swallowed the whole efficient market theory—Sharpe, market line, and beta.

As Lorie and Hamilton (who like all three forms) point out:

> If these startling hypotheses are true, their practical importance is enormous. They would profoundly affect security analysis, portfolio management, and the selection of an investment strategy.

Although they concede that "one cannot assert for certain whether these hypotheses are true or not," they "confidently assert" that the evidence regarding their validity is "persuasive," and they leave no doubt that they themselves are indeed persuaded.

This Is Evidence?

We are indebted to Lorie and Hamilton especially for their review of the supporting evidence, because they have covered the literature much more thoroughly than we have, and we thought we might have missed something essential. The evidence is even weaker than we had supposed, and we'll cite examples following this summary definition of the hypothesis:

> An efficient market is one in which a large number of buyers and sellers react through a sensitive and efficient mechanism to cause market prices to reflect fully and virtually instantaneously what is knowable about the prospects for the companies whose securities are being traded.

Other True Believers would omit the qualifying and inexact word *virtually* and say flat-out that price adjustment, even to "anticipated" information, is instantaneous. No matter; even their own evidence shows that price adjustment does take time.

One study reviewed by Lorie and Hamilton, that of Eugene Fama and others, and offered in support of the semistrong hypothesis, involved the effect of stock splits on stock prices. It was apparently intended to explode the "folklore with respect to stock splits . . . that the total value of an issue of common stocks was increased by increasing the number of shares." (Our research has not uncovered any folks who believe that a split pie is any bigger than it was in its original state.)

> The study covered 940 stock splits during a 34-year period and the estimated relationship of monthly rates of return on individual stocks to that of all stocks listed on the NYSE.
>
> The estimated relationships are based on the 420 months during the 1926–60 period with the exception of the 15 months before and the 15 months after the month of the split. These months were excluded because unusual price behavior in months surrounding the split would obscure the long-term relationship.

Thus the "unusual price behavior" lasting months and months was excluded from a study apparently intended to back up the "instantaneous price adjustment" of an "efficient market."

Another study cited is one by Raymond J. Ball and Philip Brown intending to prove the equally inane proposition that most earnings information has been discounted before it finally appears in annual reports:

> They found that the average rates of return for stocks with "increased earnings" [relative to the market] rose throughout the year preceding the announcement. For stocks with "decreased earnings," the opposite was true.

What else, indeed, would one expect? The price changes were due to earnings forecasts (in which True Believers don't believe) as well as quarterly earnings reports and other relevant events. Note that prices changed "throughout the year," *not* instantaneously, but in the usual pattern of overadjustment and underadjustment resulting from varied, incomplete, faulty, and emotional analysis of news—real and imaginary—by people with a wide variety of reflexes, few if any of them instantaneous.

In support of the "strong form" of the hypothesis, Lorie and Hamilton cite studies by Irwin Friend and others at the Wharton School, and by William Sharpe, John Lintner, and Michael C. Jensen, which generally conclude that "even the professional managers of mutual funds failed consistently to outperform a comprehensive market index." We believe all this to be useful and probably authentic information, but we do not believe that it proves that "the capital market is highly efficient." Knowing something of how these professionals operate, and the constraints to which many of them are subject, we have to congratulate them for doing as well as they did.

Moreover, most studies of this type show that a few mutual fund managers (the exceptions so annoying to modcaps) do better than average on a fairly consistent basis. That only a few excel is to be expected. The large sample that mutual fund managers represent in the total market *can't be expected to perform better than the average.* They are not, on average, supermen. They are, sad to say, only average.

Disbelief

Charles P. Jones, in his "Earnings Trends and Investment Selection," describes the "basic" random-walk theory in terms approximating the "weak" form, and the "broad" one in terms similar to the "semistrong" form. Living proof that an academician need not be a True Believer, he writes:

> We believe that the stock market is not as perfect as some proponents of the broad random walk theory maintain. That is, publicly available information does not appear to be fully discounted as soon as it becomes available. We postulate that there is a knowledge gap between investors and that the non-professional investor is unable to analyze new information concerning the fundamental worth of common stocks as efficiently as a professional.[34]

While his postulate on just who is responsible for the gap may be arguable, one certainly exists, and the result is a market that is less than efficient.

The Jones article finds support for the hypothesis "that quarterly earnings reports significantly better than anticipated by market professionals tend to generate intermediate stock price trends."

As Frank E. Block has pointed out in the article cited earlier describing "the dichotomy between academicians and practitioners," the latter:

> cannot agree with those academic views which assume the presence of markets which are "in equilibrium" and "efficient markets". . . . Either concept would tend to support the random walk adherents' belief that investment analysis can obtain no better than random results without inside information or other special advantages.[6]

Even the last qualification is denied by the strong form discussed above.

In fact, those who are really close to the stock market are not about to accept the efficient market theory in any form—strong, lame, or halt. The man who is running the world's biggest securities market, James Needham, chairman of the New York Stock Exchange, obviously does not think even the Big Board is efficient; he is worried about its very liquidity,[15] which of course is one of the prime requisites of any market that professes efficiency.

All practitioners know that there never has been a stock market without overpricing and underpricing. Even the Big Board has been getting less efficient recently because of restricted liquidity, caused both by the individual investors' flight from the market and the institutional investors' concentration on a relatively few issues.

"My most important source of information," admitted a Boston portfolio manager to *Business Week* ("A Gamble with Billions"), "isn't Wall Street research. It's what the bank trusts are buying."[10]

That is the sort of informed professional opinion upon which the efficient market rests.

Summing Up

This final chapter was aimed at exposing two more major fallacies of modern capital market theory, namely, that the stock market is an efficient market, in which stock prices adjust immediately to reflect all available information; and the related fallacy, also stemming from the random:walk theory, that it is impossible to beat the market.

This entire book, in fact, has been aimed at exposing the fallacies of modcaps and other faddists and demonstrating, we think, an alternative method that investors can believe in and profit by. If the reader has been paying attention, no further elaboration should be necessary . . . except, perhaps, a short Epilogue (which follows), occasioned by ongoing developments.

EPILOGUE

EVEN AS the modern capital market theorists gain adherents, contrary evidence is accumulating. *Fortune,* which in June 1973 wrote that their studies showed that the "wrong" (meaning the low-beta) stocks had provided the highest returns the year earlier, editorialized the following month "It's Time to Buck the Two-Tier System," suggesting that the way to do so was to follow the lead of the academicians and such banks as Wells Fargo by investing in some market index such as the Standard and Poor's 500.

We protested in a letter to the editors that doing so would simply result in a somewhat different two-tier market. They thanked us and printed (in the September issue) the part of our letter commending the lead article, "How the Terrible Two-Tier Market Came to Wall Street," along with our prediction that Morgan's Law would take care of the lofty price/earnings "vestal virgins" on which the institutions were concentrating—a process which was well under way before the issue hit the stands.

However, they omitted our criticism of the editorial giving support to the modcaps, and our comment that the academic evidence is not "overwhelming," as they said, but *under*whelming and contradictory; and also our opinion that "the fact that some banks are actually selling this idea [that you can't beat the averages, so the wisest policy is to join them] to pension, profit-sharing, and other trust funds is an indication of how confused the investment world is right now."

Well, you can't win them all.

Modern capital market theory is also heating up in the *Financial Analysts Journal,* as the latest issue (July 1973) gives evidence, with four articles bearing closely on the subject.

Most disturbing to the modcaps should be R. Minturn Sedgwick's "The Record of Conventional Investment Management," which shows that although most of the common stock and endowment funds he studied failed to beat the S & P 425 industrials over substantial time periods, some, in fact, *did:* 5 out of 24 mutual funds (21 percent) in the 12-year period December 31, 1960 to December 31, 1972, when the index showed a growth rate of 9.5 percent; and 3 of the 36 college endowment funds (8 percent) in the 10-year period June 30, 1961 to June 30, 1971 (with two more funds tying the 8 percent growth rate of the index).

These figures are more than statistical "outliers"; they are very significant by any statistical standard. And although they give no comfort to the efficient market adherents, they are in accord with our thesis that only a few can excel.

Sedgwick's article sings the praises of his plan for investing in the "20 largest" industrial companies—revising the list every two or three years, and assuming "reasonable operating costs," the same 0.2 percent he applies to the S & P index for comparison. Over the 24-year period December 31, 1948 to December 29, 1972, the 20-largest fund outperformed the index 14.3 percent annually to 13.4 percent, indicating that the index *can* be beaten over a very long time period, and—remarkably—by a very "naive" or "brute force" method.

No doubt the modcaps would like more details (and so would we). Modcaps might also protest their policy of trading as little as possible would result in even lower costs than the 0.2 percent assumed, but the 20-largest approach is itself very close to "buy and hold" because the list requires little revision. Moreover, management *fees* for the "index funds" are no lower than those for conventional trust funds.

We must note that the 20-largest approach seems to give empirical if not theoretical backing to the current concentration of institutional investors on a relatively few "vestal virgins," which in turn has resulted in "the terrible two-tier market." We, of course, do not advocate this approach, for we believe that our system of portfolio management, with buy and sell timing based upon the quantification of risk and opportunity, can produce results which are far superior.

Another article in the same issue of the *Journal,* "Risk Measurement: Five Applications," by Richard A. Crowell, concludes, also *contra* modern capital market theory, that although beta is one factor to consider in portfolio management, earnings forecasts and other aspects of securities research are also important.

Finally, a rather curious twist was applied to the capital asset pricing model by Robert S. Kaplan and Roman L. Weil, in "Risk and the Value Line Contest," appearing in the same *Journal.* The authors selected two portfolios based upon their "belief in the efficient market hypothesis," one with the highest betas which would do well in an up market, and the other with the lowest betas which would perform relatively well in a down market.

As it happened, the market, as measured by the Value Line index, dropped 8.78 percent during the contest period August 18, 1972 to February 16, 1973. The *relative* performance of both portfolios was as predicted: the high-beta set placed in the lowest 0.6 percent of all entries in the contest, and the low-beta set in the top 2.3 percent. In a down market, the low-beta portfolio should have moved lower also; however, it moved *counter* to the market, advancing 3.8 percent.

"To explain how this can be expected to happen," wrote the authors, "requires some algebra. The standard asset pricing model states that the *expected* return on a portfolio, $\bar{R}_p$, is given by $\bar{R}_p = (1 - \beta_p)R_f + \beta_p\bar{R}_m$ where β_p = systematic risk of the portfolio, R_f = rate of return on the risk-free asset, and $\bar{R}_m$ = expected rate of return on the entire market. The equation shows that when β_p is negative or merely small, $\bar{R}_p$ can be positive even when $\bar{R}_m$ is negative because the risk-free asset, such as a six-month U.S. Treasury bill, yields a positive return."

This seems to present another example of True Believers going out of their way to show their devotion to the cult. *There were no risk-free assets* in their portfolio or in the Value Line contest—and not even dividends were considered in calculating price appreciation, so the explanation did nothing to explain what actually happened.

The authors could well have used the model attributed to Fischer Black, Michael C. Jensen, and Myron S. Scholes in the Lorie and Hamilton book[42] already referred to. In similar terminology it would read, $\bar{R}_p = (1 - \beta_p)R_z + \beta_p\bar{R}_m$, where the only difference is that R_z, the return on a portfolio having *no* coordination with the market, has been substituted for R_f, the return on a risk-free asset.

Of course, it might well be that Kaplan and Weil are in essential agreement with Black, Jensen, and Scholes, and that the latter meant their R_z, like R_f, to represent only the return on a risk-free asset. But let's be a bit more imaginative and assume that R_z represents *any* part of a portfolio (including stocks) that does not conform to beta.

What the formula says then, of course, is that while one part of a portfolio may neatly conform to the "standard" capital asset pricing model, the other part can go its own merry way, independent of the model. That is precisely what happened in the case of the low-beta portfolio; while part of it no doubt went down obediently along with the market, enough of the rest of it bucked the trend so that there was a net gain for the total portfolio.

If all theorists would accept this version of the model, along with its broadest implications, the gap between them and the practitioners will be considerably narrowed (one of our goals, you recall).

Our own approach, as we have seen, goes much farther, incorporating the dynamic factor, current price, into the measurement of risk and opportunity.

GLOSSARY

Beta or Beta Coefficient: A measure of the variability of rate of return (or, rarely, price) of a stock or portfolio compared to that of the overall market. This is a very useful concept, but its usefulness has been largely frustrated by the modern capital market theorists' emphasis on rate of return (rather than price) and the introduction into beta theory of such unnecessary, unrealistic and obfuscating assumptions as risk-free rate of lending and borrowing, available to all investors.

The Poor Boy beta (see definition) is more useful and more easily calculated, even though it has the drawback (from the modcaps' point of view) that it is understandable by the ordinary investor and fund manager.

Capital Asset Pricing Model or Efficient Market Model or Market Line Theory: The main conclusions evolving from this body of theory are as follows (after the excellent summary by Vasicek and McQuown[69]):

1. Optimal investment opportunities consist of combinations of a risk-free asset and one particular portfolio of common stocks. (The theory assumes that the investor can borrow or lend at the same risk-free rate.)

2. The investor can select any degree of risk desired by adjusting the proportions of the risk-free asset and the stock portfolio, even borrowing at the risk-free rate to increase the stock holdings.

3. The greater the risk assumed, the greater the expected rate of return.

4. Although each investor must decide what risk level he is willing to assume, he need not select particular stocks nor be concerned with combining them into a portfolio.

5. Every investor's stock holdings should consist of a part of the same

portfolio, namely the "market portfolio," which "comprises all the shares outstanding of all the common stocks in the market."

6. All portfolios consisting of any other combinations of stocks, or any single stock, will have a lower expected return—for a given level of risk—than a portfolio consisting of the market portfolio and the risk-free asset.

7. "The market does not compensate for unnecessary risk, i.e., risk that can be diversified away." [In other words, "you can't beat the market," and the only perfectly diversified portfolio is the entire market, or one which moves in perfect lock-step with it.]

8. The total risk of a security or portfolio consists of (*a*) systematic risk, due to its covariance with the market and (*b*) specific risk, due to any variability which is independent of market fluctuations.

9. The expected rate of return on a security or portfolio is solely a function of its systematic risk; the higher the systematic risk, the higher the expected return.

10. Perfectly diversified portfolois have no specific risk, "and they represent investment opportunities superior to all other combinations of assets."

11. The beta of a security or portfolio is its systematic risk expressed in units of market risk. The expected rate of return of any security or portfolio is determined solely by its beta, "thus promoting beta to the most important single characteristic of any security or portfolio." Beta is defined as the "covariance of a stock or portfolio with the market, divided by the variance of the market itself." In least squares regression analysis, beta is the "slope coefficient in the regression of the security's rate of return on the market rate of return."

Although the "efficient market model was developed under some simplifying assumptions concerning zero transaction costs and rapid information dissemination . . . the empirical findings to date tend to conform to the implications of the model . . . [and] it has been shown that the basic conclusions of the model hold under much more general assumptions."

Covariance: The degree of related movement between two variables, such as the price or rate of return of two stocks. It is measured by summing the products of the differences of each pair of observations from their averages, and dividing by the number of paired observations:

$$\text{Covariance} = \frac{\Sigma(X - \bar{X})(Y - \bar{Y})}{n}$$

where:

$$\bar{X} = \text{Mean of the } X \text{ measures}$$
$$\bar{Y} = \text{Mean of the } Y \text{ measures}$$
$$n = \text{Number of paired measures}$$

In a portfolio consisting of several stocks, covariances tend to cancel each other, so the covariance of the portfolio (with the market, say) is less than the sum of the covariances of the individual stocks. This is generally considered to be the desirable effect of diversification.

Current Price Factor: The measure of overpricing or underpricing used in this book (see Chapter 5 for derivation):

$$\text{Current price factor} = 2 \times \frac{\text{Price} - \text{Average price}}{\text{Average price}}$$

Dispersion: The spread or variability (see definition) of random individual values around their mean or average.

Efficient Market: The efficient market model describes the state of equilibrium of what are assumed to be efficient capital markets. "A perfectly efficient market is one in which new information is immediately and costlessly available to all investors and potential investors, and the cost of action (transaction costs, taxes, etc.) is zero."[69]

The stock market is considered by modcaps to be close enough to this perfect one so that "each common stock is, at any moment, priced fairly with respect to its value." They argue that information channels are efficient, investors react very quickly to perceived changes in "value," their buying and selling quickly results in the appropriate price adjustment, and—lo!—the price is *right* all the time. Backing this up with empirical studies, the modcaps insist that "the principle of efficiency holds very closely," and "all currently available information about future prices is discounted in today's price."[69]

Efficient Portfolio: One having the highest expected return for its particular risk level; or one having the lowest risk for a given level of expected return.

This definition is sound if a measure of real risk is intended. However, modcaps equate risk with variability, without consideration of current price; therefore, they would deny the possibility that a portfolio of underpriced stocks could be more efficient, and have a higher expected return, than another portfolio of less variable but overpriced stocks.

Expected Rate of Return and Expected Value: These are tricky concepts when applied to the stock market. Although expected value (which results from weighting all possible outcomes by their probabilities) has a well-deserved place in statistical science, its application to the market is made difficult by the fact that both outcomes and probabilities are based in the final analysis on subjective judgments. Modern capital market theorists, moreover, would have us believe that when the market drops, say, 20 points in a day that (1) all investors' expectations have uniformly dropped proportionately and (2) their judgment is *right.* It should be obvious that the expected and the real coincide only on rare occasions, and then only by chance, when a stock is going from overpriced to underpriced, or vice versa. Expected rate of return is further complicated by the variety and difficulty of defining rate of return, and measuring it even when all of the information is available.

Market Sensitivity: The average amount of price change experienced by a security or portfolio in response to a change in the general market. Price sensitivity can be most readily measured by dividing price range variability of a security or portfolio by that of the market, as defined by some broad market index.

Modcaps measure market sensitivity by beta (see definition), a measure of variability in rate of return.

Mean Absolute Deviation: A measure of variation or dispersion which is calculated by first determining the average of all observations or projections (e.g., of rates of return), and then the absolute difference between each observation and the average (regardless of whether it is positive or negative), and finally summing the differences and dividing by the number of observations:

$$\text{Mean absolute deviation} = \frac{\Sigma[X - \bar{X}]}{n}$$

Model: Classy name for an idea, hypothesis, formula, or method, especially if one is not quite sure what it is.

Modern Capital Market Theory or Modcap: Derives from the theory and models originating importantly with Markowitz and developed by Sharpe and the followers of both. It includes the subjects discussed under Capital Asset Pricing Model (see definition), with which it is often equated, efficient markets, efficient portfolios, expected rates of return, and systematic and specific risk and their measurement. The random-walk theory developed into, and is still basic to, modern capital market theory.

Opportunity: This, the counterpart of risk, is exposure to the possibility of gain due to a rise in price. Opportunity is measured by the formula developed in Chapter 5, and it consists of two elements, range variability and the current price factor. A method for giving proper weight to dividends, which are usually of only minor importance in enhancing opportunity, is described in Chapter 7.

In most technical writings on the subject of risk, the term *opportunity* is not used, and therefore not distinguished from risk, which is equated with "uncertainty." Uncertainty contains elements of both risk and opportunity, which must be clearly distinguished in order to be measured. In the literature, the concept of opportunity is generally—and inadequately—expressed by the term *reward* (see definition).

Overpriced: This is the condition of a security when it is selling at prices higher than can be justified on the basis of such criteria as "intrinsic value," "expected value," or projected average price. In terms of risk and opportunity measurement, a security is overpriced whenever risk exceeds opportunity, and the degree to which it is overpriced can be measured by the current price factor or the risk/opportunity ratio. A high risk/opportunity ratio represents a selling opportunity, and a low R/O ratio, a buying opportunity.

Poor Boy Beta: A simple measure of price variability, or volatility, of a stock or portfolio compared to that of the overall market, as measured by some broadly based index. It is calculated by dividing the range variability of a stock or portfolio by that of the market. For example, the price of a stock with a Poor Boy beta of 2 will, on average, move 2 percent (up or down) with every 1 percent move of the market (in the same direction). A negative beta indicates movement counter to that of the market.

Range Variability: The measure of price volatility used in this book. It is the difference between the high and the low (the range) divided by the average price.

Reward: Usually understood to mean rate of return, or expected rate of return (see definition).

Risk: As the term is used in this book, risk is exposure to the possibility of loss due to a drop in price. Risk is measured by the formula developed in Chapter 5 and consists of two elements, range variability and the current price factor. A method for giving due weight to dividends, which are usually of only minor importance in moderating risk, is demonstrated in Chapter 7.

In most other writings on the subject, risk is equated with uncertainty, or unpredictability about the future, and it is quantified by some statistical measure of variability, commonly mean average deviation, variance, or standard deviation. This book shows that these concepts are inadequate, mainly because (1) "uncertainty" and "variability" contain opportunity as well as risk, and the two must be clearly distinguished, and (2) current price, as well as variability, must always be considered in measuring risk.

The confusion about the real meaning of risk is unfortunate, not only because it has impeded the measurement of risk, but because it forces the reader constantly to keep in mind what the writer means by "risk." Since most of theoreticians are actually talking about variability, which contains both risk and opportunity, the word *risk* in their works might well be replaced by *variability,* or perhaps *varisk,* at least in the mind of the reader.

Risk-Aversion: A state of mind that varies widely among individual investors according to such factors as liquidity and consumption requirements, their respective time horizons and, quite possibly, their degree of ignorance about just what risk-aversion actually means. Investors generally are considered by economists to be risk-averse; that is, to "prefer more stable holdings to less stable ones, other things being equal,"[69] (but things never are).

Risk-aversion plays an important role in the efficient market model, for it is believed that the actions of market participants, trading off their individual needs for income and the corresponding degrees of risk, result in the "appropriate" pricing of risky assets. The model, however, defines risk as uncertainty or variability and ignores current price—a large detail of which every market participant is acutely aware.

To be consistent, those who define risk as variability should also use the term *variability-aversion.* This might perhaps lead them to agree that variability does indeed have two elements, risk and opportunity; and no market participant is averse to the latter.

Risk/Reward Ratio: A term in common use (and a legitimate, though ill-defined, one) which indicates the tradeoff inherent in all investment situations between the reluctance to part with one's money and the greedy desire to multiply it. Modern capital market theorists share the desires of ordinary investors in wanting to minimize risk while maximizing reward. The theorists' quest is complicated unnecessarily by their own definitions of risk and reward. The risk/opportunity ratio is on sounder ground.

Sharpe Diagonal Model: Much as we are disinclined to give space here to formulas not of our own making, we feel that in all fairness we owe one to the modern capital market theorists. Here is their favorite, by the "Father of Beta," a model expressing, for a given time horizon, the return on a security (R_s) as a function of the risk-free rate of return (R_f) plus beta times the return on the market (βR_m) plus a return, alpha, peculiar to the security:

$$R_s = R_f + \beta R_m + \alpha$$

Both alpha and beta are measures of variability, which is only a partial measure of risk (or opportunity). The Sharpe model, like that of Markowitz, is a static one, because it makes no allowance for current price, buying, and selling. As every investor knows, real return depends upon the prices at which stocks are bought and sold. That is why the risk/opportunity model has a current price factor.

Specific Risk: The risk attributed to the characteristics of a specific stock, i.e., those unrelated to overall market movements. Modcaps believe that alpha (specific risk) and beta (market-related risk) together measure total risk, and that the former, unlike the latter, is not compensated by the market, because it can be eliminated by portfolio diversification. They also relate dividends to market risk, in spite of their obvious ties to specific companies.

Standard Deviation: Also called mean square deviation, this is a common measure of variation or dispersion which is calculated by taking the square root of the variance (see definition):

$$\text{Standard deviation} = \sqrt{\frac{\Sigma(X - \bar{X})^2}{n}}$$

Standard deviation, like all other measures of variability, is a useful measure for statisticians, but an inadequate measure of risk.

Systematic Risk: The risk due to the response of a stock to changes in the overall market. Modcaps believe that the market compensates for taking systematic risk with a proportional return, and that specific risk (see definition) is not so compensated because it can be eliminated by diversification. Systematic risk is also called market-related risk and market sensitivity, and it is measured by the beta coefficient.

Uncertainty: The modcaps equate this with risk, but uncertainty is not *all* bad, since it can also represent the opportunity for gain resulting from a price rise.

Underpriced: This is the condition of a security when it is selling at prices lower than it should be on the basis of such criteria as "intrinsic value," "expected value," or projected average price (which we use in this book). All securities are underpriced about half the time. In terms of risk and opportunity measurement, a stock is underpriced whenever opportunity exceeds risk, and the degree to which it is underpriced is indicated by the current price factor and the opportunity/risk ratio.

Variability: The modcaps equate this, as they do uncertainty, with risk, and they quantify it with such statistical measures as mean absolute deviation, variance, and standard deviation. Variability contains elements of both risk and opportunity, which must be clearly defined in order to be measured usefully.

The basic variability measure used in this book as a partial measure of risk and opportunity (along with the current price factor) is range variability.

Variance: A statistical measure of variation or dispersion that is calculated by determining the average of all observations (e.g., of rates of return), the differences between each observation and the average, summing the squares of the differences, and dividing by the number of observations:

$$V = \frac{\Sigma(X - \dot{X})^2}{n}$$

Standard deviation is the square root of variance. Both are inadequate measures of risk.

Volatility: The term is best restricted to mean price variability (as it is, in fact, commonly understood by almost all investors and portfolio managers). It should not be applied, as it is by modcaps, either to variability in rate of return or to market-related rate of return—which, for clarity, should be called exactly by those names.

This book uses range variability to measure volatility.

BIBLIOGRAPHY

1. Ahlers, David M. "SEM: A Security Evaluation Model." *Analytical Methods in Banking.* Edited by Kalman J. Cohen and Frederick S. Hammer. Homewood, Ill.: Richard D. Irwin, Inc., 1966.
2. Black, Fischer. "Capital Market Equilibrium with Restricted Borrowing." *Journal of Business,* July 1972.
3. ———. "Implications of the Random Walk Hypothesis for Portfolio Management." *Financial Analysts Journal,* March 1971.
4. ———; Jensen, Michael C.; and Scholes, Myron. "The Capital Asset Pricing Model: Some Empirical Tests." *Studies in the Theories of Capital Markets.* Edited by Michael C. Jensen. New York: Praeger Inc., Publishers, 1972.
5. ———, and Scholes, Myron. "Dividend Yields and Common Stock Returns: A New Methodology." *Proceedings of the Seminar on the Analysis of Security Prices.* Chicago: University of Chicago Press, November 1970.
6. Block, Frank E. "Elements of Portfolio Construction." *Financial Analysts Journal,* May 1969.
7. Blume, Marshall E. "On the Assessment of Risk." *Journal of Finance,* March 1971.
8. ———. "Portfolio Theory: A Step toward Its Practical Application." *Journal of Business,* April 1970.
9. Bogle, John C. "Mutual Fund Performance Evaluation." *Financial Analysts Journal,* November 1970.
10. *Business Week.* "A Gamble with Billions." March 31, 1973.
11. ———. "One Born Every Minute." April 14, 1973.
12. ———. "Optimal Control: A Mathematical Supertool." May 10, 1973.

13. ———. "The Spreading Scandal at Equity Funding." April 14, 1973.
14. ———. "What If They Don't Come Back?" June 1, 1973.
15. ———. "Jim Needham: What's Wrong with Wall Street." April 14, 1973.
16. Cohen, Kalman J., and Hammer, Frederick S. *Analytical Methods in Banking.* Homewood, Ill.: Richard D. Irwin, Inc., 1966.
17. Diefenbach, R. E. "How Good Is Institutional Brokerage Research?" *Financial Analysts Journal,* January 1972.
18. Dietz, Peter O. *Pension Funds: Measuring Investment Performance.* New York: Free Press, 1966.
19. Dorfman, Dan. "Heard on the Street." *Wall Street Journal,* April 19, 1973.
20. Douglas, George W. "Risk in the Equity Market: An Empirical Appraisal of Market Efficiency." *Yale Economic Essays,* Spring 1969.
21. Fama, Eugene. "Efficient Capital Markets: A Review of Theory and Empirical Work." *Journal of Finance,* May 1970.
22. ———. *Risk and the Evaluation of Pension Fund Portfolio Performance.* Park Ridge, Ill.: Bank Administration Institute, 1969.
23. ———; Fisher, Lawrence; Jensen, Michael C.; and Roll, Richard. "The Adjustment of Stock Prices to New Information." *International Economic Review,* February 1969.
24. Ford Foundation Advisory Committee on Endowment Management. *Managing Educational Endowments.* New York: The Ford Foundation, 1969.
25. *Fortune,* "The Strange News about Risk and Return." June 1973.
26. Graham, Benjamin. *The Intelligent Investor.* 4th rev. ed. New York: Harper & Row, 1973.
27. ———; Dodd, David L.; and Cottle, Sidney. *Security Analysis: Principles and Technique.* New York: McGraw-Hill, 1962.
28. Granger, C. W. J. "What the Random Walk Model Does NOT Say." *Financial Analysts Journal,* May 1970.
29. Harbrecht, Paul P. *Pension Funds and Economic Power.* New York: The Twentieth Century Fund, 1959.
30. Hartwell, John F. "Performance: Its Promise and Problems." *Financial Analysts Journal,* March 1969.
31. Innocenti, Robert E. "The Stock-Bond Split Decision for Pension Funds." *Financial Analysts Journal,* November 1969.
32. Jensen, Michael C. "Risk, the Pricing of Capital Assets, and the Evaluation of Investment Portfolios." *Journal of Business,* April 1969.
33. ———. "The Foundations and Current State of Capital Market

Theory." *Studies in the Theory of Capital Markets.* New York: Praeger Inc., Publishers, 1971.

34. Jones, Charles P. "Earnings Trends and Investment Selection." *Financial Analysts Journal,* March 1973.
35. Kaplan, Robert, and Roll, Richard. "Accounting Changes and Stock Prices." *Financial Analysts Journal,* January 1973.
36. Laing, Jonathon R. "Bye-Bye Go-Go? More Money Managers Now Aim Just to Match Popular Market Indexes." *Wall Street Journal,* June 7, 1973.
37. Levy, Robert A. "On the Short-Term Stationarity of Beta Coefficients." *Financial Analysts Journal,* November 1971.
38. Lintner, John. "The Aggregation of Investors' Diverse Judgment and Preferences in Perfectly Competitive Security Markets." *Journal of Finance and Quantitative Analysis,* April 1970.
39. ———. "The Valuation of Risk Assets and the Selection of Risky Investments in Stock Portfolios and Capital Budgets." *Review of Economics and Statistics,* February 1965.
40. Lorie, James H.; Cohen, Kalman J.; Dean, Joel; Durand, David; Fama, Eugene F.; Fisher, Lawrence; and Shapiro, Eli. *Measuring the Investment Performance of Pension Funds for the Purpose of Inter-Fund Comparison.* Park Ridge, Ill.: Bank Administration Institute, 1968.
41. ———, and Fisher, Lawrence. "Some Studies of the Variability of Returns on Investment in Common Stocks." *Journal of Business,* April 1970.
42. ———, and Hamilton, Mary T. *The Stock Market: Theories and Practices.* Homewood, Ill.: Richard D. Irwin, Inc., 1973.
43. Markowitz, Harry M. "Portfolio Selection." *Journal of Finance,* March 1952.
44. ———. *Portfolio Selection: Efficient Diversification of Investments.* New York: John Wiley & Sons, 1959.
45. Miller, F. Byers, and Robinson, Randall S. *A Management Summary of Measuring Investment Performance of Pension Funds for the Purpose of Inter-Fund Comparison.* Park Ridge, Ill.: Bank Administration Institute, 1968.
46. Morton, Walter A. "Risk and Return: Instability of Earnings as a Measure of Risk." *Land Economics,* May 1969.
47. Murphy, John Michael. "The Value Line Contest: 1969." *Financial Analysts Journal,* May 1970.
48. O'Brien, John W. "How Market Theory Can Help Investors Set Goals, Select Investment Managers and Appraise Investment Performance." *Financial Analysts Journal,* July 1970.

49. Osborne, M. F. M. "Brownian Motion in the Stock Market." *Operations Research,* March 1959.
50. Richardson, Lemont K. "Do High Risks Lead to High Returns?" *Financial Analysts Journal,* March 1970.
51. Robinson, Randall S. "Measuring the Risk Dimension of Portfolio Performance." *Journal of Finance,* May 1970.
52. ———. "The Measurement of Investment Performance." *Profit Sharing Magazine,* December 1969.
53. Rustin, Richard, and Meyer, Priscilla. "How the Word Spread about Equity Funding." *Wall Street Journal,* April 9, 1973.
54. Securities and Exchange Commission. *Institutional Investor Study Report.* Washington, D.C.: U.S. Government Printing Office, 1971.
55. Sharpe, William F. "A Simplified Model for Portfolio Analysis." *Management Science,* January 1963.
56. ———. "Capital Asset Prices: A Theory of Market Equilibrium under Conditions of Risk." *Journal of Finance,* September 1964.
57. ———. *Portfolio Theory and Capital Markets.* New York: McGraw-Hill, 1970.
58. ———. "Risk, Market Sensitivity and Diversification." *Financial Analysts Journal,* January 1972.
59. ———, and Cooper, Guy M. "Risk-Return Classes of New York Stock Exchange Common Stocks." *Financial Analysts Journal,* March 1972.
60. 'Smith, Adam.' *The Money Game.* New York: Random House, 1967.
61. Soldofsky, Robert M. "Yield-Risk Performance Measurements." *Financial Analysts Journal,* September 1968.
62. Thomas, Conrad W. "Beta Mousetrap? There's a Simple and Practical Way of Measuring Risk." *Barron's,* February 7, 1972.
63. ———. "Hedging Does Work: The Technique Is Better Than Some Who Claim to Use It." *Barron's,* October 4, 1971.
64. ———. *Hedgemanship: How to Make Money in Bear Markets, Bull Markets and Chicken Markets While Confounding Professional Money Managers and Attracting a Better Class of Women.* Homewood, Ill.: Dow Jones-Irwin, 1970.
65. ———. "Primer for Shorts: How to Survive and Even Prosper in a Bear Market." *Barron's,* November 2, 1970.
66. Tobias, Andrew. "The Best Put-Down Artist on Wall Street." *New York,* February 5, 1973.
67. Treynor, Jack L. "How to Rate the Management of Investment Funds." *Harvard Business Review,* January 1965.

68. ———; Priest, William W.; Fisher, Lawrence; and Higgins, Catherine A. "Using Portfolio Composition to Estimate Risk." *Financial Analysts Journal,* September 1968.

69. Vasicek, Oldrich A., and McQuown, John A. "The Efficient Market Model." *Financial Analysts Journal,* September 1972.

70. Wagner, W. H., and Lau, S. C. "The Effect of Diversification on Risk." *Financial Analysts Journal,* November 1971.

71. *Wall Street Journal.* "SEC Senses Advisor Who Analyzes by ESP Had Defrauded Public." May 7, 1973.

72. Welles, Chris. "The Beta Revolution: Learning to Live with Risk." *Institutional Investor,* September 1971.

73. Wetzler, James W. Letter commenting on the article, "The Value Line Contest: 1969." *Financial Analysts Journal,* September 1970.

74. Whitbeck, Volkert S., and Kisor, Manown, Jr. "A New Tool in Investment Decision-Making." *Financial Analysts Journal,* May 1963.

75. Williamson, J. Peter. "Computerized Approaches to Bond Switching." *Financial Analysts Journal,* July 1970.

76. ———. "Measurement and Forecasting of Mutual Fund Performance: Choosing an Investment Strategy." *Financial Analysts Journal,* November 1972.

77. Wynn, Wilton. "The Mind-Splitting Job of Running Montedison." *Fortune,* April 1973.

INDEX

N

O

P

Q–R